Courtroom and Report Writing Skills for Social Workers

Other titles in the Post-Qualifying Social Work Practice series

Advanced Social Work with Children and Families ISBN 978 1 84445 363 4
The Approved Mental Health Professional's Guide to Mental Health Law (2nd edition)
ISBN 978 1 84445 115 9
The Approved Mental Health Professional's Guide to Psychiatry and Medication
(2nd edition) ISBN 978 1 84445 304 7
Critical Thinking for Social Work (2nd edition) ISBN 978 1 84445 157 9
Effective Leadership, Management and Supervision in Health and Social Care
ISBN 978 1 84445 181 4
Evidence-based Policy and Practice in Mental Health Social Work (2nd edition)
ISBN 978 0 85725 425 2
Introducing Child Care Social Work: Contemporary Policy and Practice
ISBN 978 1 84445 180 7
Law and the Social Work Practitioner (2nd edition) ISBN 978 1 84445 264 4
The Mental Capacity Act 2005: A Guide for Practice (2nd edition) ISBN 978 1 84445 294 1
Newly Qualified Social Workers: A Handbook for Practice ISBN 978 1 84445 251 4
Practice Education in Social Work: A Handbook for Practice Teachers, Assessors and
Educators ISBN 978 1 84445 105 0
The Practice Educator's Handbook ISBN 978 085725 094 0
Proactive Management in Social Work Practice ISBN 978 1 84445 289 7
Social Work Practice with Adults ISBN 978 1 84445 292 7
Values and Ethics in Mental Health Practice ISBN 978 1 84445 375 7
Vulnerable Adults and Community Care (2nd edition) ISBN 978 1 84445 362 7

To order, please contact our distributor: BEBC Distribution, Albion Close, Parkstone, Poole,
BH12 3LL. Telephone: 0845 230 9000, email: **learningmatters@bebc.co.uk**. You can also
order online at **www.learningmatters.co.uk**.

Courtroom and Report Writing Skills for Social Workers

Second edition

CLARE SEYMOUR AND RICHARD SEYMOUR

Series editors: Steve Keen and Keith Brown

LearningMatters

First published as Courtroom Skills for Social Workers in 2007 by Learning Matters Ltd.

Reprinted in 2009
Second edition published in 2011

British Library Cataloguing in Publication Data
A CIP record for this book is available from the British Library.

ISBN: 978 0 85725 409 2

This book is also available in the following formats:
Adobe ebook ISBN: 978 0 85725 383 5
EPUB ebook ISBN: 978 0 85725 382 8
Kindle ISBN: 978 0 85725 384 2

Cover and text design by Code 5 Design Associates Ltd
Project management by Deer Park Productions, Tavistock
Typeset by Pantek Arts Ltd, Maidstone, Kent
Printed and bound in Great Britain by Bell & Bain Ltd, Glasgow

Learning Matters Ltd
20 Cathedral Yard
Exeter EX1 1HB
Tel: 01392 215560
info@learningmatters.co.uk
www.learningmatters.co.uk

Contents

Foreword

Welcome to the Post-Qualifying Social Work Practice Guides by Learning Matters. We have designed these guides to be full of practical tasks, ideas and guidance, making them ideal for the busy social worker, or indeed those training to be social workers. It is our sincere desire that they help the social work profession to reach even higher standards and ultimately benefit people who use services, and carers.

As part of the Post-Qualifying Social Work Practice series, these Practice Guides have been written by people with a passion for excellence in social work practice. This publication is no different. The other books in the series may also be of value to you as they are written to inform, inspire and develop social work practice.

Dr Steven Keen and Professor Keith Brown (University of Bournemouth Centre for Post-Qualifying Social Work)

About the authors

Clare Seymour is a registered social worker. Until 2009 she was Senior Lecturer in Social Work at Anglia Ruskin University, where she taught social work law, communication and interviewing skills, and professional accountability to social work students at undergraduate and master's level. Her social work experience includes 16 years of local authority children's social work, where she had wide experience of court work, and bereavement support within a general practice. She is currently working with social work students as a practice educator, and as an external examiner.

Richard Seymour is a Senior Circuit judge assigned to the Queen's Bench Division of the High Court of Justice. He was in practice as a barrister until 2000, was appointed QC in 1991, and has been a President of Mental Health Review Tribunals. He jointly edited *Kemp & Kemp, the Quantum of Damages*, 4th edn, 1975, and contributed the legal chapters to publications on practice and procedure for the quantity surveyor, and the architect in practice.

Acknowledgements

We have received valuable assistance from professionals who undertake different roles in court, and from two people who have shared their personal experiences of social workers and courts. We express our warmest thanks to the following:

Barbara Armitage, Dave Barron, Christopher Compston, Hazel Davies, Jane Day, Diana Eaglestone, Amy Gordon, Sue Kettlewell, Alison Lamont, Ann Milne, Dot Neville, Corné Van Staden, Laura and Michael (not their real names). We are also very grateful to John Noyce who prepared the diagrams.

Introduction

Michael's only child was removed from his care and, ultimately, placed for adoption. He agreed to talk to us about his experiences, expressing the hope that it would contribute to the training of social workers in the future.

CASE STUDY

Michael's story

One day, I came home to find two social workers in my living room. They always come in pairs so you're immediately outnumbered. Intimidating is putting it mildly, though later it was always me who was described as intimidating. Looking back, I'd lost the battle the day they got involved in my life. The more I fought to keep my daughter, the more hostile they became and the more they looked for things to use against me. Nothing I could say or do made any difference – as a parent, I was completely powerless.

My partner had left me with our seven-month-old daughter and before I realised what was happening the social workers decided she wasn't safe with me. They based everything on what they'd been told by her mother. They didn't check anything out – there were no questions, no investigation, nobody talked to my neighbours or anyone who knew me, they took everything at face value and I was categorised and stereotyped from the start. Before I came to England I worked in security and I've always been interested in martial arts, but apparently that made me a bad parent. How does owning a collection of ornamental knives make me a violent person? Even my dog was held against me, although he's never hurt anyone.

After my daughter was taken away, I went to a solicitor, who gave me a rundown of what would happen. However, he didn't tell me it would go on for two and a half years. I didn't realise that not all solicitors are experts in child law and I've also learned that if you've got problems with the council, don't use a local solicitor. They're all pally with each other and after court the solicitors and social workers all went to lunch together. You feel completely left out on a limb.

The children's guardian is supposed to represent the interests of the child, but when my daughter dislocated her arm while in foster care, the guardian told me it was 'just an accident', as if that made it OK. I can imagine what would have been said if it had happened while I was looking after my daughter. During the whole of the court proceedings, the guardian only saw me with my daughter twice, each time for less than half an hour. How can that show her what kind of parent I am?

I always had to make an appointment to speak to the social worker and he never returned my calls. He was negative towards me from the start and had made up his mind that I

Continued

1

wasn't a good parent. In one report he described me as 'an aggressive black man'; if I'd described him as 'a dishonest white man' it would have been considered racist. No one told me when a new social worker took over – I first met him at court. He didn't last long and a third one appeared. The guardian said I should 'give her a chance'. By this time there were files full of reports – what social worker is going to have time to read them all from start to finish? As a result she made mistakes and said things in court which weren't true. She never came to see me with my daughter and relied on reports from the contact supervisors, who changed quite often so no one had a complete picture. I agreed to go to parenting classes and D, the person who ran the classes, sent a report to the social worker. However, what the social worker put in her evidence bore no relation to what had actually happened. Fortunately D had sent me a copy of her report and so the social worker came unstuck when cross-examined in court. If it hadn't been so serious, it would have been funny – she looked like a fish out of water, totally dumbfounded and embarrassed. However, the magistrates carried on regardless and, as usual, sided with the social worker.

I just couldn't trust the social workers. Everything seemed to happen behind my back. They made my ex-partner sign an agreement not to return to me, telling her it was just an informal arrangement, but then it appeared as evidence in the court documents, handwritten on a scrap of paper. Another time I had my arm in plaster because I'd fallen downstairs after tripping over the cat. This was then presented by the social worker as me having been hurt in a fight. It was no good me denying it – I was always in the wrong. They seemed determined to gather as many negative points as possible, and weren't concerned whether or not they were true. Because I didn't trust them, I wouldn't allow them to see my medical records, but this made me 'uncooperative and failing to engage'. I wasn't supposed to know where my ex-partner was living, but when she took my daughter from the contact centre without permission, the social workers came straight round to ask me to help find her. Then the council included her address in some court documents I was sent. It was close to my home, so we couldn't avoid meeting occasionally and there was sometimes overlap at contact. However, this apparently showed that we were 'in an enmeshed relationship'. Luckily I could understand most of their jargon, but not everyone would be able to.

After the final hearing, I received a letter from the council. There was no 'Dear...', and it was headed 'Re: reduced contact schedule in relation to MJ born 12/4/2008', as if I don't know my daughter's date of birth or needed to be told what the letter was about. After listing the dates I could see my daughter 'until an adopter is found', it finished with 'Your co-operation is greatly appreciated', as if I had a choice. Obviously the person who wrote that letter never gave a moment's thought to, or didn't care, how I might be feeling at the prospect of losing my daughter for ever. After three years they've only just started looking into my complaints, which of course is too late for me and my daughter.

This book is for social workers and social work degree students who wish to develop their courtroom and recording skills. It supports the QAA subject benchmarks and National

Occupational Standards for social work and addresses areas of competence required by newly qualified social workers. It also meets specialist standards and requirements for post-qualifying social work education and training in relation to work with children, young people, their families and carers (GSCC, 2005).

Commentators have suggested that relationships between lawyers and social workers can be strained, characterised by mistrust or even antagonism (Preston-Shoot et al., 1998, cited in SCIE, 2005; Dickens, 2006), and that social workers often regard the law as intimidating, confrontational and more likely to be obstructive than empowering (Preston-Shoot, 2000). Despite the shared commitment to justice, honesty and transparency, many social workers feel uncomfortable about perceived differences in the professional value bases of law and social work, and indeed the need to invoke the law at all to resolve social issues. Studies (Dickens, 2006; Beckett et al., 2007) also suggest that to social workers court proceedings can seem like a game, in which service users' needs become sidelined or obscured altogether. Our aim is to demystify court processes and help you to regard court work as a positive element of your practice, rather than something to be afraid of or defended against (SCIE, 2005). In encouraging you to become more confident, analytical and, if necessary, critical, we hope that you will be better equipped to support service users facing court proceedings.

Although few social workers see themselves as key players in court (Beckett and McKeigue, 2010), they need to be able to communicate effectively with lawyers, judges, magistrates and children's guardians, both in their own interests and those of service users. By learning the 'rules of the game' and developing the skills required, you are not compromising the values of your profession; rather, you are establishing yourself as an equal partner in the court setting, which provides the opportunity to influence events and potentially make a difference to the experience of service users. Since records and reports are the means by which much of your practice is exposed to external scrutiny, we have explored the particular challenges you will face in this context. However, specialist knowledge and technical skills are not enough; you also need to develop the confidence and independence of thought to question the organisation and purpose of legal rules, and to analyse critically the social context of our court systems (SCIE, 2005, page 16). Much legal decision-making involves balancing one person's rights or opinions against another's within a complex framework, influenced by a range of principles and sources. The core skills that social workers can contribute to these decisions include:

- Knowledge – about disability, attachment, loss, human development, mental health, abuse, poverty or neglect.

- Skills – in advocacy, assessment, analysis, risk management, research, report writing and working with others.

- Values – partnership, self-determination, choice, confidentiality, accountability, honesty, transparency, fairness and commitment to social justice.

Throughout the book there are activities, diagrams, case studies, research summaries and reflections from professionals who work in courts, and from people with personal experience of our legal system. All are intended to offer practical information and advice to support your continuing professional development.

Part 1
The English legal system in context

Chapter 1
Historical development

This chapter will help you to meet the following National Occupational Standards for social work.

- Key role 6: Demonstrate professional competence in social work practice.
  - Review and update your own knowledge of legal, policy and procedural frameworks.

Introduction

As English law embarks on a period of radical reform and challenge, its longer-term history is becoming an increasingly important topic.

(Baker, 2002, page 1)

Part of the apprehension which non-lawyers feel when involved with legal processes stems from unfamiliarity with, and lack of understanding of, the English legal system. Not only does its terminology still tend to be obscure, despite recent moves to address this, but the way in which it has developed has produced a system which can appear illogical and confusing. In explaining the present organisation of our courts and legal profession, we are reminded of the proverbial advice to the lost motorist: 'If I were you, I wouldn't start from here'. The United Kingdom of Great Britain and Northern Ireland comprises the four countries, England, Wales, Scotland and Northern Ireland. So why is there not a United Kingdom or British legal system? As so often in puzzling aspects of national life, the answers lie in history.

Review your knowledge, skills and learning needs:

- *Where has your present knowledge of our legal system come from?*
- *What experiences have you had of law generally?*
- *What experiences have you had of the legal framework of social work?*
- *What do you think will help you develop confidence in working within this legal framework?*

English common law

Most people think of law as something which results from Parliament having debated an issue and then passed an Act. However, before the 1066 Norman invasion of England, law did not exist in the form in which it does now. England, Wales, Scotland and Ireland were then separate countries and laws in England, such as they were, were more like customs, developed to regulate society. Different parts of the country produced different laws and customs, partly because during the previous Anglo-Saxon period England was divided into several kingdoms. In 1066, what we think of as the law was not regarded as distinct from other aspects of society. Local courts, which had existed since Anglo-Saxon times, dealt with all types of public business, including settling disputes and punishing offenders. However, successive Norman kings, starting with Henry II, decided to set up central, Royal courts, concerned only with the administration of justice. The courts which developed as a result are the predecessors of the courts we have today, which explains both why the legal system is as it is and some of the unusual names still in use.

The decision to have central courts also explains how English law has developed. In order to operate effectively, the Royal courts required one legal system in place of the variety of local laws and customs. It was necessary, therefore, to have a *common law* applicable to everyone, which is how English common law came about. For lawyers, *common law* has a number of meanings. As we have seen, historically it is the law applicable to the whole of England. In another sense it is law which is not written down in Acts of Parliament but which is found in the decisions of judges over the last thousand years. Unsurprisingly, early records are sketchy, but since the sixteenth century judges' decisions have been recorded in law reports. A decision made 500 years ago is not often referred to today, but occasionally it does happen. Because this part of our law is based on custom, in theory it has always been the same, which means that when judges decide a case on the principles of the English common law, they are not making new law, but are revealing what the law has always been.

Donoghue v. Stevenson [1932] AC 562

Look up the details of this case – which involves a snail and a bottle of lemonade – in a law library or on the internet. Although it dates back around 80 years, the Appeal Court's decision established a legal principle in relation to negligence which still stands today.

The existence of English common law, in the sense of law which is not contained in Acts of Parliament, has had two effects which are important to the development of the English legal system:

- Unlike almost every other country, the United Kingdom has no written constitution.

- The most fundamental principles of English law are not found in Acts of Parliament, but in decisions of judges.

A written constitution usually includes the creation of a court system, provision for the appointment of judges and a definition of their powers. The Acts of Parliament which deal with various courts and tribunals in England are all fairly recent in the context of their history; the first to deal with the higher courts was passed in 1873, 700 years after the first attempts to establish a central court system. All of the Acts of Parliament which affect what is now the High Court have been passed on the assumption that that court has what is called *inherent jurisdiction*, which means no more than the jurisdiction which the predecessors of the High Court had always had. But to discover what this is, again we need to look at their history.

In countries like France or Germany, where all laws are written down, or *codified*, the function of judges is limited to interpreting the law and applying it to the facts of a particular case. However, in England, because so much important law is not found in Acts of Parliament, and because the powers of the High Court are not precisely defined, the role of judges in the High Court is possibly more important than that of judges in countries with codified laws. There is one important exception, however; in countries with a written constitution, there is sometimes a court, like the Supreme Court of the United States of America, which has the power to overrule, as being unconstitutional, laws passed by the equivalent of Parliament. No court in England has that power.

The third sense in which lawyers use the expression *common law* is to distinguish between the type of law called equity, and law which is not equity. However, in this context common law can, confusingly, include statute. We look at equity later in this chapter.

The development of central courts – the initial stages

In the early Middle Ages, the principle became established that the source of justice was the king, who consequently had to ensure that justice was delivered to his citizens. This was partly achieved by the king taking control of local courts, but a system also developed of officials being sent around the country to supervise royal officials, collect taxes and settle grievances. In 1178 Henry II, deciding that permanent officials were needed to decide disputes, set up a group of five members of his household, two of whom were clergymen, whom he instructed to *hear all the complaints of the realm and to do right*. This body then evolved into a permanent court, the Court of Common Pleas. The name *court* came from those assembled round the king, his court, and *pleas* simply meant claims. Although no longer used in this sense, the word *plea* is still used in criminal courts to indicate whether or not defendants admit their guilt. *Common* meant between subjects of the king, rather than cases in which the king had an interest. Initially, the Court of Common Pleas had to refer difficult cases to the king for him to decide, in consultation with what were called the wiser men of the realm, and so in effect it was possible to appeal to the king against a decision of the Court of Common Pleas.

In addition to the cases referred to the king and the wiser men of the realm, there were also disputes which involved the king. It was inconvenient for him personally to be involved in all these decisions and so, by the beginning of Edward I's reign, these types of case were dealt with by a group of professional judges known as the Court of King's Bench. The name came from the fact that the judges were exercising the king's functions as the ultimate judge of the country. The court had close relations with the king's council and the king continued to be involved with its decisions until the reign of Edward III. The role of the king as the ultimate judge explains why the final court of appeal was, until the creation of the Supreme Court in 2009, the House of Lords, which had taken over the king's judicial functions in hearing appeals.

The Court of Common Pleas and the Court of King's Bench no longer exist. They and the third common law court, the Court of Exchequer, which originally was concerned with financial matters, were amalgamated in 1873 into what is now the High Court. Initially, each of these former courts survived as a Division of the High Court, and as Queen Victoria was on the throne the Court of King's Bench became the Court of Queen's Bench. In 1881 the three Divisions were amalgamated into the Queen's Bench Division, which remains a Division of the High Court. Although at first the courts of Common Pleas and King's Bench travelled around the country as the king progressed from place to place, they soon became based permanently in Westminster, and the higher courts remained in Westminster Hall until the Royal Courts of Justice opened in the Strand, London in 1882.

Deciding the facts in the Court of Common Pleas was entrusted to juries, whose members were expected to come from the county where the particular dispute arose. Initially, once the Court of Common Pleas became established in Westminster, each jury had to go there. However, it soon became clear that it was easier to send the judges to the jury. Other types of judicial business, in particular serious criminal trials, also involved judges travelling around the country, and so the judges began to undertake all the necessary business in the county to which they were despatched, which was the origin of the *assize system*. Hearings outside London took place in assize towns, which were, at the time, the principal towns of the country. Today High Court judges still sit in crown courts in some of the old assize towns, such as Lewes in Sussex, which may be less notable than places nearby. During the Middle Ages, travel was not easy and it made sense for judges to visit other places in the area before returning to London, which is how assize circuits developed. The country is still divided for legal purposes into circuits, of which there are now six. Most barristers are members of a circuit, circuits continuing to have some significance for the administration of the courts and the assignment of judges to particular areas.

Judges appointed in the reign of Henry II were referred to as *justices* and High Court judges are still called *Mr Justice* or *Mrs Justice*. For some reason the title *Miss Justice* for unmarried female judges has never been used.

Juries

The jury as we know it is quite different from how it operated originally. The jury's current role is to hear the evidence and decide the facts in crown court criminal trials or, sometimes, at inquests or, more rarely, in civil trials of libel, slander, or false arrest or imprisonment actions. Originally juries were not meant to be independent assessors of evidence; they were summoned because they were supposed to have prior knowledge of the facts. Until the end of the nineteenth century, juries decided the facts in both civil and criminal cases. They have lost this role in respect of most civil cases and the function which they still have in libel cases, and other limited categories, is all that is left of a much more influential role in the justice system.

Coroners

If you have ever wondered why there has to be a coroner's inquest into a sudden or suspicious death, or how coroners came to be involved with questions of treasure trove, the answer is money. Citizens were potentially liable to a fine if a Norman died in unexplained circumstances, and the coroner's original function was to ensure that the king received any fines due to him as a result of such deaths and any abandoned treasure to which he was also entitled.

Local criminal courts and the origin of magistrates

Most people are familiar with magistrates' courts as the lowest level of court and know that those who preside over them are sometimes referred to as justices of the peace, a title dating back to the Justices of the Peace Act 1361, passed during the Hundred Years War with France. During a break in the fighting, demobilised English soldiers started roaming the country causing trouble and the original justices of the peace were worthy local citizens appointed in each district to restore and maintain order. Originally they received salaries from the fines they imposed, but as their value declined, the salaries were not worth collecting and have long been obsolete. Whether that fact is relevant or not, justices of the peace were considered to do such a good job in dealing with crime at a local level that they have continued to carry out the same functions for over 650 years.

As justices of the peace had no legal qualifications, their jurisdiction and powers were limited. However, they were not only a court. Before elected county and district councils were established at the end of the nineteenth century, local government was managed by justices of the peace who met four times a year to decide important matters at *quarter sessions,* which came also to include legal business. They sat with a legally qualified chairman and had more powers than when they were sitting alone, in what were called *petty sessions.*

Chancery

One of the present Divisions of the High Court is the Chancery Division, the origin of which was the Court of Chancery, incorporated into the High Court in 1873. The word *chancery* is a contraction of *chancellery,* the department of the Chancellor, or, in England, the Lord Chancellor. Under the Constitutional Reform Act 2005, the Lord Chancellor ceased to be head of the judiciary, a position which he had held for over 900 years. How did he come to have that role in the first place?

The Lord Chancellor was always an important royal official as Keeper of the King's Conscience. In the Middle Ages few people other than clergymen were literate, so most civil servants were clergymen. The courts of Common Pleas and King's Bench were both what is called *common law courts*, in that the law they applied was the English common law. In time the way in which cases were dealt with came to depend on compliance with strict rules so that a case could be lost because the rules had not been followed correctly, even if the case was otherwise a good one. People thought this was unfair and some complained to the king. The Lord Chancellor, in his role as Keeper of the King's Conscience, therefore developed an approach to disputes which ignored the strict rules and concentrated on what was thought to be fair, or *equitable*. Initially it was said that what the Lord Chancellor decided was equitable varied with the length of his foot; in other words, there were no set principles or consistency. However, gradually the rules became standardised and known as *equity*. Like English common law rules, they are not written down but are found in cases reported in law reports. The court in which a person could seek equity was the Lord Chancellor's Court, the Court of Chancery. In effect, equity trumped common law rights and you could go to the Court of Chancery to obtain an order preventing someone from taking advantage of a common law right in a common law court, which was useful in some cases.

The ecclesiastical courts and the origins of the Family Division

In the Middle Ages the state was not concerned with family matters. Marriage, the ending of marriage and the consequences of death were of no interest to the king, except in relation to the passing of property rights, which affected the operation of the feudal system. At first, grants of land by the king to lords were for life and the land reverted to the king on the lord's death. However, later, landowners could leave their property to whomsoever they liked. The state had no continuing interest in this and so marriage and wills were dealt with by the church. At that time there was no possibility of divorce; theoretically a marriage could be annulled, but the process was complicated and expensive. Disputes about these matters were determined in church courts, which still exist within the Church of England although they now have limited jurisdiction in relation to clergymen and church buildings. Church courts did not apply the English common law or the principles of equity to resolving disputes, but principles derived from the law of the church. This meant the law of the Roman Catholic Church, which applied throughout Western Europe and was heavily influenced by the law of the Romans.

Starting from the Reformation in the reign of Henry VIII, the state became more interested in matters which had been left to church courts. First, wills came within the sphere of the Court of Chancery. In the eighteenth century Parliament began to intervene in reg-ulating marriage, followed by legislation governing how wills should be made. An Act of Parliament permitting divorce in very limited circumstances was passed in 1857, and a divorce court was established which was amalgamated into the High Court in 1873 as part of what was then the Probate, Divorce and Admiralty Division, which is now the Family Division. Subsequently family matters came increasingly within the jurisdiction of the ordinary courts.

County courts

County courts existed in Anglo-Saxon times, but today's county courts were established by the County Courts Act 1846. Initially, anyone wanting to pursue a civil claim, whatever the amount involved, had to initiate the action in London, which was very inconvenient. Local county courts were therefore introduced to deal with the recovery of small debts and demands. Over time, the jurisdiction of county courts has increased and they now deal with a wide range of civil and family matters.

Crown courts

After the creation of the High Court, judges of the Queen's Bench Division and the Probate, Divorce and Admiralty Division, but not the Chancery Division, continued to try serious criminal cases at assizes. Cases which were less serious, but still too serious to be dealt with by magistrates, were tried by quarter sessions. These two systems were com-bined by the Courts Act 1971 which established crown courts, where all serious criminal cases are now tried.

Court of Appeal

The Civil Division of the Court of Appeal was established by the Judicature Act 1873 which provided for all appeals from county courts and the High Court to be heard by one court. This situation has now changed, with most appeals from county courts heard by a High Court judge. The Court of Appeal did not hear appeals in criminal cases until the Court of Criminal Appeal was established in 1907. In 1968 it merged with the Court of Appeal, which now has civil and criminal divisions, with the same judges sitting in either division as required.

The Supreme Court

The Supreme Court, which opened for business in 2009, was created by the Constitutional Reform Act 2005 to supersede the judicial functions of the House of Lords. The role of the House of Lords as a court, as well as part of Parliament, dated back to when the king was the fount of all justice and if you thought someone had done you a wrong, the person who could put it right for you was the king. When supreme power became vested in Parliament, which took over the role of the monarch, not only in relation to making new laws but also as the source of redress for anyone who felt that they had not achieved justice through other courts, the ultimate court of appeal became Parliament, specifically the House of Lords. In time the non-legally qualified members of the House of Lords came to appreciate that they should defer to those with appropriate legal knowledge and experience. Initially they consulted the judges before making decisions, but later senior judges were made Law Lords in order to deal with the legal business which came to the House. At first, non-legal members could also take part, but from 1881 only judges appointed to the House of Lords could decide cases. The judges of the new Supreme Court are specifically appointed to that role.

ACTIVITY 1.3

- *What does a comparison of the historical development of our legal and social welfare systems (see Figure 1.1) tell you about the differences and similarities between them?*

- *What effects, if any, do you think these historical influences are likely to have on the way in which the legal and social work professions operate today?*

Local customs and laws before	1000	
	1100	
Court of Common Pleas	1200	
Juries		
Court of King's Bench	1300	
Court of Exchequer		
Assize System established		
Litigants' helpers appeared		
1361 Justices of the Peace Act	1400	
	1500	
Law Reports record judges' decisions		
	1600	1601 Poor Law – parishes responsible for own 'deserving' poor
	1700	1795 Berkshire magistrates devised Speenhamland system of poor relief based on wage level, marital status, number of children and price of bread
1845 Law Society founded	1800	1834 Poor Law Amendment Act required
1846 County courts established		parishes to build workhouses with strict regimes
1857 First divorce court		1869 Charity Organisation Society
1873 High Court and Court of Appeal established		1871 Poor Law Board became part of local
1876 First Law Lords appointed		government
1882 Royal Courts of Justice opened		1889 Prevention of Cruelty to Children Act
1894 General Council of the Bar founded		
1907 Court of Criminal Appeal established	1900	1907 Probation of Offenders Act
		1926 Adoption Act
		1933 Children and Young Persons Act
1949 Legal Advice and Assistance Act –		1948 Children Act, National Assistance
foundation of legal aid system		Act and inception of Welfare State
1968 Court of Criminal Appeal merged into Court		1954 First generic social work course
of Appeal		1970 Local Authority Social Services Act
1971 Crown courts established		1971 CCETSW regulates social work training
1999 Access to Justice Act – Legal	2000	2000 Care Standards Act
Services Commission to manage legal aid		2001 GSCC regulates social work
2007 Legal Services Act		2003 Inception of social work degree
2009 Supreme Court established		
Legal Services Board created to oversee	2010	Health Professions Council to take over
regulation of lawyers		regulatory function of GSCC

Figure 1.1 *Development of legal and social welfare systems*

Advocates

The combination of the complexity of the rules to be followed to obtain a remedy in the common law courts, the particular rules of the Court of Chancery, and the limited literacy of most citizens meant that people came forward to help litigants to present their cases. Initially they offered their services free, but it soon became expected that helpers should receive a reward from grateful litigants, although in theory this was not a fee, but an *honorarium*, or gift. These litigants' helpers were the forerunners of modern barristers, and barristers' gowns still have a small flap on the back from which a tape runs across the shoulder to hang down the front. This flap was originally a bag on a tape which barristers held out behind them in court in order to receive the present from the grateful client. The principle that barristers acted for free and only received gifts from their clients prevailed until recently and barristers could not sue for unpaid fees. However, the principle was moderated by the fact that it was professional misconduct for solicitors who instructed barristers not to pay them the agreed fee.

Once a profession of litigants' helpers – barristers – became established, they had to be trained and regulated, which led to the establishment of the Inns of Court. Aspiring barristers had to show that they were suitable for acceptance by the Inn and discipline was exercised by senior members who were usually judges, known as Masters of the Bench, or Benchers. From the seventeenth century, the right to appear as an advocate in the Royal Courts was restricted to members of an Inn. The surviving Inns of Court are the Inner Temple, the Middle Temple, Lincoln's Inn and Gray's Inn, which have been in their present locations in London since the sixteenth century. The Inns also provided, and still do to an extent, residential and professional accommodation for their members.

As compared with barristers, solicitors are newcomers on the legal scene, although they had respectable predecessors, scriveners and attorneys. In the United States of America, the term 'attorney' is still used for any type of practising lawyer, but it is no longer used in that sense in England. Towards the end of the eighteenth century, solicitors emerged as the dominant branch of the non-advocacy part of the legal profession. Their function was to prepare formal legal documents, give legal advice and instruct barristers to appear as advocates in court, or to give specialist advice. They were, and still are, the first point of contact for people seeking legal advice in many circumstances. Originally, anyone wishing to be represented or advised by a barrister first had to consult a solicitor. There are now exceptions to that rule, but most people who are advised or represented in court by a barrister will first have consulted a solicitor. Formerly it was unusual for solicitors to appear as advocates in court and they had no right to appear, or *right of audience*, in the higher courts. Now solicitors can qualify as advocates and present cases in the higher courts.

Why is the legal system, and the law, English?

Wales was not part of the territories governed by the king of England until the end of the thirteenth century and was not therefore involved in the earlier development of the English common law or in the initial establishment of courts in England. After the Battle of Bosworth Field in 1485, the Tudor dynasty, which had origins in Wales, came to the English throne. It was felt in Wales that, in respect of legal processes, the Welsh were disadvantaged as compared with the English and so, in a notable act of positive discrimination, Henry VIII persuaded Parliament to make Wales part of England by law. Thereafter English law was applied in Wales in place of the preceding customary law, and for legal purposes Wales has been part of England since 1536.

From 1603 the king, or queen, of Scotland was also king, or queen, of England, but the monarchies were not united and the kingdoms were separate until 1707. Scotland had therefore developed its own legal system, based on Roman law, and its own court structure. Neither of these was altered when the kingdoms became united, which has remained the position, except that the Supreme Court is the final court of appeal in Scotland as it is in England. This is why English law applies in England and Wales, but not in Scotland, and the court structure in England and Wales is different from that in Scotland.

Ireland was first invaded from England, or, more accurately, from Wales, in 1169. From then on a presence of Normans, English and Welsh spread throughout the country and English law was applied to the parts of Ireland controlled by the English king. The law which applied in Ireland was modified by laws passed when there was a Parliament in Dublin, but in 1801 Ireland joined the United Kingdom. For the next 120 years, Parliament in London passed laws applicable only to Ireland, as well as laws which applied throughout the United Kingdom. In 1922 the Republic of Ireland became independent, with Northern Ireland remaining in the United Kingdom. At times Northern Ireland has had its own Parliament and passed its own laws, but, as in the case of the Republic of Ireland, the laws and structure of its courts remain similar to those of England. These laws are not English law, however, and therefore the next chapter concerns the legal system of England and Wales.

FURTHER READING

Baker, J H (2002) *An introduction to English legal history* (4th edition). London: Butterworths.

This text traces the development of the principal features of the English legal system which helps explain the operation of the present system.

Chapter 2

The English legal system in practice

This chapter will help you to meet the following National Occupational Standards for social work.

- Key role 1: Prepare for, and work with individuals, families, carers, groups and communities to assess their needs and circumstances.

  ○ Assess needs, risks and options taking into account legal and other requirements.

- Key role 6: Demonstrate professional competence in social work practice.

  ○ Review and update your own knowledge of legal, policy and procedural frameworks.

Introduction

Here we explore the nature and responsibilities of courts and lawyers and the relationships between them, encouraging you to develop an ability to undertake an informed and critical assessment of the operation of the English legal system. We also briefly consider future developments.

ACTIVITY **2.1**

Review your current knowledge and learning needs:

- *What experience have you had of courts?*

- *In which areas of court work do you feel most, and least, confident?*

- *In what circumstances have you wished you knew more about courts?*

- *What barriers do you think you may face in developing courtroom skills?*

- *What might help you overcome these barriers?*

Organisation of the courts

The English legal system is big business. Her Majesty's Courts and Tribunals Service (HMCTS), an executive agency of the Ministry of Justice, has 21,000 staff and operates from around 650 locations. It is responsible for the work of more than 30,000 magistrates and judges, plus supporting staff, who deal with around 2 million criminal prosecutions, 1.8 million civil claims, more than 150,000 family law disputes and around 80,000 tribunal cases annually.

HMCTS aims to ensure that:

> *All citizens receive timely access to justice according to their different needs, whether as victims or witnesses of crime, defendants accused of crimes, consumers in debt, children at risk of harm, businesses involved in commercial disputes, or as individuals asserting their employment rights or challenging the decisions of government bodies.*

There are 116,000 solicitors, nearly half of them female, and more than 14,000 practising barristers, of whom around one-third are female. Approximately 10% of each profession is from minority ethnic goups.

Courts deal with either or both of the two main divisions of legal work, criminal and civil. Criminal courts are where people who are accused of crimes either admit them, or are tried and, if found guilty, have a penalty imposed. Civil courts provide a means for people to seek remedies for injustices they think they have experienced. Family law, including divorce, adoption and child protection, is part of civil law, although the criminal law can be invoked in these contexts if it is also alleged that a crime has been committed, as is possible in cases involving domestic violence or ill-treatment of a child. Courts which make initial decisions – courts of first instance – should be distinguished from those which review the decisions of other courts – appeal courts. Some types of case in which the legal issues may be similar, for example disputes about children or responsibility for accidents, are dealt with by one court rather than another because of their level of importance or the amount of money at stake. However, these categories are not absolute because some courts have both civil and criminal jurisdiction and some courts make initial decisions and also hear appeals.

Courts have three primary roles, which reflect society's values in one form or another:

- To provide a fair and independent mechanism for upholding the values which society regards as important, including the means by which actions considered to be harmful or undesirable are discouraged and punished.

- To define fair processes for the transaction of business and regulation of human relationships, and to provide for the determination of disputes between people who are unable to resolve them independently.

- To provide a safeguard against the abuse of power, in the form of impartial scrutiny of decisions, and a means of redress if necessary.

The English court system is essentially a bottom-heavy hierarchy, with magistrates' courts at the base, over which are crown and county courts, followed by the High Court, the Court of Appeal, and ultimately the Supreme Court (See Figure 2.1).

Magistrates' courts

For over 650 years magistrates have undertaken the greater part of judicial work and around 95% of court business is conducted in some 350 magistrates' courts in England

and Wales. There are over 29,000 magistrates, evenly divided as to gender, with around 8% from ethnic minority groups. Magistrates are unpaid, other than expenses, and do not need formal qualifications, though they receive training. In addition to sitting in court, magistrates are expected to respond to urgent requests, such as warrants for arrest and search or emergency protection orders, and to take declarations of various kinds.

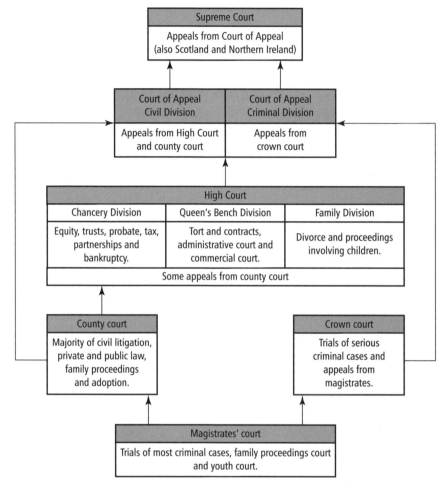

Figure 2.1 Outline of court structure in England and Wales

Local advisory committees make recommendations for appointment to the Lord Chancellor and applications are *welcomed from people from all walks of life who have the quali-ties and the time to serve as magistrates*. The age range for holding an appointment is 18–70, although anyone over 65 is unlikely to be newly-appointed. In terms of gender, ethnic origin, geographic spread, occupation and political affiliation, each bench is required broadly to reflect the community it serves. However, perhaps unsurprisingly in view of the time commitment and the fact that the position is unpaid, magistrates are likely to be middle-aged and middle-class people who are prominent in their local community through business, professional or charitable activities. Usually magistrates sit in threes, and for youth and family courts there must be a mix of gender. All magistrates have equal decision-making powers but only the chairperson communicates directly with people in court.

Some magistrates' courts in larger cities, where there is a high volume of business, are presided over by district judges (magistrates' court), who are full-time paid professional judges. There are also deputy district judges (magistrates' court), barristers or solicitors in practice who are paid for sitting part-time as judges. Because magistrates are not legally qualified, they are guided on the law by a qualified clerk.

Magistrates' courts deal with both criminal and civil matters. In criminal cases, their role is to decide the facts by assessing the evidence, and to determine the sentence for anyone who is found guilty. Magistrates' courts are divided into adult and youth courts, with the latter responsible for cases involving young people between the ages of 10 and 17. Youth courts are less formal than adult courts, both in relation to layout and the way in which proceedings are conducted, and hearings take place in private. The press is normally allowed to attend but the child or young person concerned must not be identified in any reports.

ACTIVITY 2.2

- *What do you think should be the age of criminal responsibility?*
- *What factors do you think are likely to influence such a decision?*
- *What possible consequences could result from it being 10, rather than 12, 14 or 16?*

The age of criminal responsibility in England, 10, is one of the lowest in Europe, which means that more young people here than in the rest of Europe have gained a criminal record by the time they become adult. However, there have been calls for the age to be raised, with the suggestion that younger children who commit crimes would be more effectively dealt with by means of a welfare-based approach managed by social care services rather than the criminal justice system (Prison Reform Trust, 2010). Scotland plans to raise its age of criminal responsibility to 12. A curious legal anomaly, dating back to the Children and Young Persons Act 1933, means that in criminal courts and police detention 17-year-olds are regarded as adults and do not receive additional protection and assistance, such as an adult's presence during police interviews, which is afforded to children under 17.

All criminal cases start, and most finish, in the magistrates' court. The few that do not are either so serious that magistrates' powers are considered insufficient to deal with them, or are offences for which the accused person has the right to ask for a crown court trial in front of a judge and jury (known as *either-way offences*). When criminal cases are transferred to a higher court, magistrates still decide matters such as whether bail is to be granted to the accused person and, if so, on what terms.

Magistrates' courts have a role in relation to some civil matters, such as council tax enforcement, and its family proceedings court deals with cases of domestic violence and disputes involving maintenance payments or the welfare of children.

Magistrates do not have robes and wear their ordinary clothes in court.

The crown court

For criminal cases, crown courts, of which there are 77 in England and Wales, are the next step up the court hierarchy. Crown courts also hear appeals from magistrates' courts against conviction or sentence (see below).

Judges in the crown court are usually full-time and salaried circuit judges, a title introduced when crown courts were established in 1971. However, the judicial system depends heavily on the assistance of part-time judges, known as recorders, most of whom are practising lawyers who are paid to sit as judges for three to six weeks each year. Anyone wishing to become a full-time judge usually first works as a part-time judge. Serious cases, such as murder, are usually tried by High Court judges, some of whom spend about half the legal year, around 18 weeks, sitting in crown courts around the country.

ACTIVITY 2.3

Crown courts and magistrates' courts are open to the public and observing them in action is a good way of developing an understanding of how courts operate. If you explain to an usher why you are there, they should be able to direct you to a court where something interesting is going on. Take care not to enter or leave a court during the swearing in of the jury or of a witness, or during the judge's summing up. Family hearings are not open to the general public but, by prior arrangement with their clerk, many judges are willing to allow people with a professional interest to observe what happens in court as part of their training and development.

County courts

The 216 county courts in England and Wales deal with almost all civil actions within their prescribed financial and legal limits, such as unpaid debts, defective goods, personal injury, breach of contract and housing disputes. Remedies which can be awarded are usually either financial (damages) or restitutional (putting right whatever was complained of). County courts also have an important role in relation to family matters, including divorce, domestic violence, adoption and local authority action to protect children. Cases are allocated to a county court designated to hear the particular type of case involved, such as a Care Centre for public law applications by local authorities, where the judges have received specialist training. As in crown courts, hearings can take place before circuit judges or recorders, but a considerable amount of county court work is undertaken by district judges, or part-time deputy district judges, who decide cases with a value less than £15,000, conduct consumer arbitrations and deal with administrative arrangements for trials.

PRACTITIONER REFLECTION **2.1**

The work of a district judge

Most of the time I sit completely alone – no clerk, police officers, or phalanxes of court staff – in the informal surroundings of my room. I'm expected to have a working knowledge of the law, practice and procedure affecting civil disputes, including contract, negligence, bankruptcy, personal injury, property and family matters. I may also have to deal with emergencies, such as applications for injunctions because of domestic violence or because a child has been snatched from a parent, or to stop building work encroaching on someone's property. Each morning, in addition to reading the day's case papers, I also deal with paper orders made in the absence of parties, such as directions for the conduct of a case, applications for adjournments or the enforcement of judgements.

Tuesdays and Wednesdays tend to be family business days. Every couple of weeks we have conciliation appointments when a family court adviser is available to assist parties in trying to resolve their differences in disputes about children. Thursdays are usually possession days when I deal with landlord and tenant matters or mortgage possessions – often more than 60 applications in one day. Friday is for road traffic accident claims. More general applications, enforcement proceedings and trials in more substantial cases are spread over other days and one of us is always designated as the 'urgent judge' to deal with matters which arise at the last minute. Add to this e-mail and conference messages, testing the new template system which enables us to draw up orders on the computer, catching up with the latest case and statute law, and meeting with the other judges to ensure consistency and you have quite a full day.

Many of the people who appear before me do not have the benefit of legal representation and, with no one to support me and minimal protection, I have to be not just knowledgeable about the law but often a social worker, psychologist and therapist as well.

From **www.judiciary.gov.uk/about-the-judiciary**, which contains accounts of the working lives of different levels of judge.

In the past the law has had a reputation for not being particularly user-friendly. However, efforts are being made to introduce a more business-like culture, particularly in civil courts. County court cases are allocated to one of three tracks, multi-track, fast track and small claims track, and are subject to case management until they come to trial or settlement is reached. Complex claims with a value over £25,000 are usually dealt with via multi-track. Fast track is for cases where the amount at stake is between £5,000 and £25,000 and the hearing, if it happens, should take no longer than a day. Claims worth less than £5,000 are assigned to the small claims track, which does not require legal representation and is intended to be a simpler, more informal way of resolving disputes. Claimants simply complete a form, which can be downloaded or submitted online, and pay a fee in order to initiate an action. Money claim online and Possession claim online are similar services for people seeking to recover money owed or possession of property.

County court hearings can be either private or public, although they do not usually invoke much public interest. Cases involving family matters and personal finances are usually heard in private, although since 2009 accredited representatives of the press have been able to attend most family court hearings, with the exception of placement and adoption hearings and those conducted for the purpose of judicially assisted conciliation or negotiation. The court can still restrict press attendance if the welfare of the child requires it, or for the protection of parties or witnesses. This decision was of concern to some social workers who often have to express opinions, or be associated with decisions, which are deeply unpopular with one or more of the parties involved. However, the principles of transparency and openness are important in the context of fairness and there was a strong lobby from user-led organisations which felt that the interests of users of family courts would be better served if the proceedings were open to public scrutiny. In practice, there has been little evidence of interest on the part of the press in reporting ordinary family hearings.

RESEARCH SUMMARY

A preliminary study of the impact of the changes to court rules governing media attendance found that a majority of court staff and stakeholders considered that resultant changes had been minimal. Three-quarters of respondents were unaware of any instances of media attendance at family hearings and few were aware of any press articles which had resulted.

(Ministry of Justice, 2010a)

Research into children's views of the family justice system found almost no support for reporters or the general public being admitted to court hearings involving the welfare of children.

(Ofsted, 2010b)

The High Court

The next tier of court is the High Court, which has three Divisions, Chancery, Queen's Bench and Family, each of which includes a Divisional Court, and, in the Chancery and Queen's Bench Divisions, some specialist courts. There is considerable overlap between the work of the Chancery and Queen's Bench Divisions, but Queen's Bench deals with more important or higher-value civil cases, such as personal injury, negligence and claims against local authorities for wrongful actions, and Chancery is concerned with matters such as trademarks and patents, bankruptcy, wills, financial regulation and disputes about trusts, land and leases. The Family Division, as its name suggests, hears more complex family law cases, including divorce, wardship, adoption, child abduction and public law proceedings under the Children Act 1989.

High Court trials take place before a High Court judge, a circuit judge sitting as a High Court judge, or a deputy High Court judge, usually a QC who is sitting as a part-time judge. Case management is undertaken, and many applications are dealt with, by junior judges, known in the Chancery and Queen's Bench Divisions as Masters and in the Family Division as Registrars.

Court of Appeal

At this level there remains a distinction between criminal and civil cases. The Criminal Division hears appeals against conviction or sentence, or both, from crown courts, and the Civil Division hears appeals in civil cases from the High Court, and some appeals from county courts.

Appeals in ordinary civil cases

In ordinary civil cases it is not possible to appeal against a county or High Court decision without permission, unless the appeal is against a committal order, a refusal to grant habeas corpus, or a secure accommodation order made under the Children Act 1989 s25. Applications for permission to appeal are made either to the court making the original order or to the court to which an appeal can be made. However, if the court making the original order refuses permission, you can apply to the court which has jurisdiction to hear the appeal. Permission to appeal is only granted if the court considers that the appeal has a real prospect of success or if there is some other compelling reason why the appeal should be heard. It is possible to give permission to appeal which is limited to specified issues.

The *real prospect of success* criterion means that most cases finish at the trial stage. It is unlikely that permission would be given to appeal in any case which depends solely upon the facts which the judge found. There is obviously a better chance of obtaining permission if there is an issue of law. If permission is granted, the appeal is normally a review of the lower court's decision. The appeal court does not usually hear any oral evidence or evidence which was not put before the lower court, although there is power to do so exceptionally. The appeal court will not allow an appeal unless the original decision was wrong, or it was unfair because of a serious procedural or other irregularity in the proceedings.

Appeals against decisions of county court district judges are heard by circuit judges in the same court. Appeals against decisions of county court circuit judges are usually heard by a single High Court judge, but in multi-track cases they are heard by the Court of Appeal. The Court of Appeal Civil Division also hears appeals from the High Court. Applications to the Court of Appeal for permission to appeal are dealt with by a single judge, but the actual appeals are heard by a panel of two or three judges. In rare cases it is possible to appeal from a decision of the Court of Appeal to the Supreme Court.

Appeals in family cases

Appeals in family cases, like appeals in ordinary civil cases, are usually by way of review rather than a rehearing, and fresh evidence can be heard only in limited circumstances. In family cases it is recognised that whatever decision the court reaches is unlikely to be completely satisfactory, but that it is unlikely that any other decision will be demonstrably better. Consequently, the court's decision should stand unless the conclusion is plainly wrong. The system of appeals from county courts and the High Court in family cases is similar to that in other civil cases. The crown court has no jurisdiction in relation to civil matters and so appeals from the magistrates' family proceedings court go to a Divisional Court of the Family Division, which comprises two High Court judges.

Appeals in criminal cases

There are two ways in which to appeal against a magistrates' court decision:

- The most straightforward is to appeal to the crown court, if it is suggested that the magistrates reached the wrong conclusion on the facts or imposed a sentence which was excessive. There is a right to appeal without permission, and the case is heard by a circuit judge sitting with two magistrates. Evidence is heard again, in effect in a second trial, but the risk for an unsuccessful defendant is that the sentencing powers are those of the crown court and their sentence could be increased.

- If it is felt that the magistrates' court has reached an incorrect conclusion of law, an alternative means of appealing is by way of case stated to a Divisional Court of the Queen's Bench Division of the High Court. The magistrates have to set out the facts which they have found and the question or questions of law which arose. The resulting arguments focus on the correctness or not of the law which the magistrates applied to the facts, and there is no right to challenge the facts found. The Divisional Court can determine what the law actually is and can modify the magistrates' decision in order to reflect that, but if a defendant wishes to challenge both the facts found and the law applied, the appropriate course is to appeal to the crown court.

The Supreme Court

In 2009 the Supreme Court replaced the House of Lords as the highest level of appeal court in the United Kingdom. In limited circumstances there can be an appeal from the Criminal Division of the Court of Appeal to the Supreme Court, which usually sits in panels of five or, exceptionally, seven Justices, so that there is no risk of a split decision.

Judicial review

This is the process by which a judge in the Administrative Court, a specialist court in the Queen's Bench Division, or the Upper Tribunal, reviews the lawfulness of a decision or action taken by a public body. This can result in a declaration that it should be considered as having no effect (*quashing* the action), or a direction that something else be done. It is concerned with the decision-making process itself, rather than the conclusion which resulted, so a public body could make the same decision again, even if it was decided that the process leading to the first decision was unlawful.

There are several possible reasons why judicial review cases seem to attract so much attention. There may be a number of different legal principles involved and it may be unclear how they interact, or which should prevail. For example, some applicants for judicial review have succeeded in suggesting that the provisions of the Human Rights Act 1998 should prevail over other rules. Another reason may be that people are now more inclined to challenge the actions of local or national government organisations. However, a significant factor, at least for local authorities, is that often there is insufficient time or resources to make decisions in accordance with all of the relevant law, and so inevitably they sometimes get it wrong.

European courts

The Court of Justice of the European Union, often called the European Court, ensures that laws made by the European Union are interpreted and applied consistently in member states. Therefore, if an issue of European law arises, a court in a member state can refer it to the European Court, whose judgement must be applied by the original court when deciding the case. Such references are not often made from English courts, but those that are usually come from the Supreme Court. When the European Convention on Human Rights was ratified by the UK in 1951, it was only binding on the government, not the courts. In 1965 the UK agreed to the citizen's right of direct petition to the European Court of Human Rights (ECtHR) in Strasbourg and until the Convention was incorporated formally into domestic legislation by means of the Human Rights Act 1998, the UK lost more cases in the ECtHR than any other country. The purpose of the Human Rights Act was to permit alleged breaches of the Convention to be tried in English courts, to ensure that English courts take account of previous decisions of the ECtHR, and to require all public authorities to act in accordance with the Convention's requirements. The ECtHR is not part of the court structure of England and Wales and cases can only be heard there after passing through all appeal processes in the UK.

The judges

We have already seen that magistrates are unpaid and not legally qualified. All other judges are paid and legally qualified, whether full- or part-time. The Lord Chief Justice is head of the judiciary in England and Wales, Scotland's most senior judge is the Lord President and Northern Ireland has its own Lord Chief Justice.

The statistics relating to the age, gender and education of judges show that the majority of them are white, male, middle-aged and privately educated, particularly in the higher courts. This partly reflects the training arrangements of the 1970s and 1980s, when it was difficult to qualify as a solicitor or barrister without independent financial support, and also the fact that working practices and career patterns at that time were not in any sense family-friendly. Of 108 High Court judges in post on 1 April 2010, only 16 were female. Three out of 37 Appeal Court judges, and one of the 11 Supreme Court judges, were female. Three High Court judges and 16 of the 680 circuit judges were from an ethnic minority background. District judges and tribunal judges are slightly more representative in terms of gender and ethnic background. Most judges on appointment are at least in their mid-40s and the retiring age is 70.

Measures have been introduced to increase diversity among the judiciary. Circuit judges and below can apply to sit part-time, there is the possibility of job-sharing, and career breaks are available. There is a work-shadowing scheme for those who are interested in applying, a DVD entitled *A day in the life of a judge* has been produced, and a dedicated website with interactive courtroom scenarios aims to make judges appear less remote. Additionally, Diversity and Community Relations judges have been appointed to develop knowledge of, and trust in, the justice system by creating links with local communities and schools.

How are judges appointed?

High Court judges, circuit judges, recorders and district judges are appointed by the Queen on the recommendation of the Lord Chancellor, and deputy district judges are appointed by the Lord Chancellor. Anyone wishing to become a district judge, recorder, circuit or High Court judge has to apply for the post, with the process managed by the Judicial Appointments Commission. Judges of the Court of Appeal and higher are appointed by a special selection panel set up by the Judicial Appointments Commission.

Who are the lawyers?

If you are legally represented in court, the person who speaks for you will be either a solicitor or barrister and, depending on the type and complexity of the case, there may be a legal team of several members. Many barristers and solicitors have a degree in law, although some solicitors now qualify academically by passing the Common Professional Examination or Graduate Diploma in Law after obtaining a degree in a subject other than law. It is also possible to train while working as a legal executive. Student solicitors then undertake the Legal Practice Course, while intending barristers follow the Bar Vocational Course. All must complete training in the vocational and practical aspects of their role by means of a solicitor's training contract or barrister's pupillage. Aspiring solicitors and barristers used to have to pay for the final stage of their training, which clearly limited access to the profession, but it is now usual for training salaries to be paid. Lawyers also have to undergo continuing professional development, the requirements of which are greatest in the first years of practice.

Barristers are known collectively as *the Bar*. This comes from the physical layout of the Inns of Court where there used to be a rail dividing student barristers from the governors of the Inn, the Benchers, and students were *called to the Bar* to be admitted as barristers. Individual barristers are sometimes referred to as *counsel,* which simply means someone who gives advice. Barristers are either junior barristers or Queen's Counsel. The designation QC indicates that a barrister is recognised as experienced and knowledgeable in a particular field (*learned in the law*), rather like a medical consultant, not that they actually advise the Queen or the government. They are also sometimes known as *leading counsel*. Most QCs are appointed around the age of 40, having been in practice for at least 15 years. The process of appointment involves the assessment of applicants by a firm of recruitment consultants and the payment of a substantial fee, whether or not the application is successful.

Traditionally, solicitors give general legal advice and prepare cases for trial by assembling documents and interviewing potential witnesses, while barristers give specialist legal advice and present cases in court. However, this distinction can be misleading as some solicitors present cases in court as solicitor advocates and are highly specialist in their field. If both a solicitor and barrister are involved in a case, in court the solicitor supplies documents and information to the barrister and takes notes, particularly while the barrister is questioning a witness or addressing the court. In complex cases, a QC may be engaged, supported by a junior barrister, and they share the task of assessing the papers, preparing the arguments to be put to the court and, usually, the questioning of witnesses and note taking at the hearing.

Most solicitors practise as partners in, or employees of, a firm, or as members, or employees, of a limited liability partnership. Some organisations, such as large companies and local authorities, employ their own solicitors and around 1,500 work for the Crown Prosecution Service. Barristers can be employed directly, but most are in private practice as sole practitioners, without partners in the business sense. Barristers' *chambers* are a set of offices, membership of which enables them to share business expenses, but not fees, with other barristers. Most chambers have business managers, called clerks, who obtain work for the barristers and negotiate fees. Historically, chambers had to be in one of the four Inns of Court in London, which influenced recruitment to the profession, but now there are barristers' chambers throughout the country.

Crown Prosecution Service

The CPS, headed by the Director of Public Prosecutions and staffed mainly by lawyers, decides whether a person should be prosecuted in court, based on evidence gathered during a police investigation and whether the prosecution is in the public interest. Once a prosecution decision is made, CPS staff prepare the case and present it in court. The police have access to out-of-hours advice from the CPS and can make prosecution decisions in relation to most road traffic offences and some public order offences.

Legal Services Commission

This agency, which incorporates the Criminal Defence Service and Community Legal Service, manages requests for legal representation at public expense. In Chapter 5 we consider how recent developments in the public funding of legal services are affecting people who are involved in, or wish to initiate, legal proceedings.

How are cases decided in court?

There are two basic approaches:

- **The adversarial approach** has historically been adopted in England and Wales. In this the court relies on each party to put forward rival arguments between which it can decide. The theory is that if it is up to the parties to try to persuade the court of the rightness of their respective positions, they will do everything possible to achieve that, and so all the relevant evidence and argument will be put before the court.

- **The inquisitorial approach** in which the court initiates and manages the enquiries which it believes are necessary in order to reach a decision. Many people feel that this approach, which is common in European courts, is more suitable in civil proceedings, particularly family cases in which confrontation and conflict are likely to compromise the prospects of a satisfactory long-term outcome. The Family Justice Review, due to report in 2011, is expected to support the move towards a more inquisitorial, conciliatory and mediation-based culture in family disputes and cases involving the welfare of children.

> *It is inaccurate to describe care proceedings as simply 'adversarial'; they are a hybrid, increasingly incorporating many inquisitorial features.*
>
> (Brophy, 2006, page vi)

Alternative dispute resolution

In cases in which society has an interest, it not usually appropriate to initiate negotiation in order to resolve the issue. If someone is accused of a crime for which they will be punished if found guilty, and they deny the offence, the scope for compromise is limited. However, in disputes over money or property, the parties may be persuaded to reach agreement in the interests of avoiding the risks inherent in a trial of the whole issue. This is the rationale behind changes in the conduct of civil litigation, given effect by the Civil Procedure Rules 1999, which emphasise the courts' role in assisting parties to civil actions to compromise their dispute. The methods available include the following:

- **Mediation** The court cannot itself, through judges, mediate and guide parties to a settlement because, if agreement is not reached, the court must decide the dispute and, if it had previously expressed a view on the merits of the case, its impartiality could be compromised. In addition to pre-trial discussions between the respective lawyers, courts therefore encourage the involvement of another party to help reach a settlement, which has led to the development of the role of professional mediator. As they expect to be paid, mediators tend to be engaged when a significant amount of money is at stake and the potential costs of a full hearing are high, but some courts operate voluntary, free mediation schemes, and mediation is widely used in family cases, such as disputes over contact with children or financial arrangements after a divorce.

- **Adjudication** This is a process in which a quicker, if less thorough, assessment is made of a case than would happen if it was heard to the bitter end in court.

- **Arbitration** This may be suitable for cases which involve the quality of goods or work. If someone buys a second-hand car and complains about its condition, an experienced and knowledgeable motor mechanic could be appointed as arbitrator and, after examining the car, offer an independent view as to whether the alleged defect was to be expected in a car of the age and type in question. Arbitration is also used when parties to a contract decide that, if a dispute arises between them, it is resolved in private. In certain sectors, such as construction and shipping, arbitration agreements are common.

RESEARCH SUMMARY

Mantle's (2001) investigation into the effectiveness of family mediation services included a survey of parents who had reached agreement during mediation, with particular focus on the experience of fathers. The parts played by mediators, lawyers and judges are explored through the eyes of parents, and the traditional assumption that court-based interventions are less likely to be successful is challenged.

Recent research into children's views of the family justice system found little enthusiasm for investigative or mediation-based decision-making. The method most favoured by young people with experience of family courts was that in which each side presents its case to the court (adversarial), which is the one currently practised.

(Ofsted, 2010b, page 15)

A major motivation behind the reforms introduced by the Civil Procedure Rules was the desire to reduce the costs of litigation, a theme we will revisit when we look at representation in court. The reforms have led to a significant reduction in the volume of civil litigation, which means that cases reach trial stage much more quickly. Around 95% of civil actions are settled before trial. The scope for compromise in family disputes involving children is more limited than in disputes about money or property. However, even then, the focus is on achieving a resolution which minimises damaging confrontation and enables the parties to work together in the future. Consequently, judges feel able to participate more actively in family cases than in other types of case.

Children and Family Court Advisory and Support Service (CAFCASS)

CAFCASS is an executive non-departmental government agency set up in 2001, with a budget of over £130 million. It is responsible for working with, and making recommendations in respect of, children involved in all types of family court proceedings. In private law its work is increasingly concerned with reducing conflict and helping parents reach agreement over residence, contact and other welfare issues. In public law, over half its caseload, 8,684 referrals in 2009/10, relates to representing children in care proceedings, with the remainder involving adoption, applications for emergency protection orders, secure accommodation orders or the discharge of care orders.

CAFCASS experienced a significant increase in the volume of its public law work after events surrounding the death of Peter Connelly in Haringey in 2007, resulting in delays in allocating cases and debate about the best way to safeguard and promote the welfare of children within family court proceedings. This is likely to be addressed within the Family Justice Review, due to report in 2011.

RESEARCH SUMMARY

Young people who had been involved in family court proceedings were asked whom they considered to be the best people to make important decisions about their future. Professionals who work with children were ranked first, followed by courts, judges and lastly panels of trained members of the public. Social workers were considered to be the most helpful in the course of the decision-making process, followed in order of helpfulness by parents, advocates, independent reviewing officers, lawyers, CAFCASS guardians, teachers, police, judges and doctors. More than half of the children surveyed stated that courts never or rarely made the right decisions about children.

(Ofsted, 2010b, page 8)

Tribunals

We went to hear a case the day before and it was fine, it was all relaxed, and we thought, it's going to be fine, so we weren't prepared for ours to be not so fine.

(Applicant to Employment Tribunal)

Tribunals are intended to offer a quicker and cheaper way of resolving disputes. Like judicial review, they also provide a means by which people can challenge the decisions of public bodies and, although they are similar to courts, they are usually less formal and make use of relevant specialist expertise. There is potential for social workers to advise, advocate for and support people at tribunals, as well as to undertake more formal roles as in, for example, providing social circumstance reports in respect of applicants who are seeking release from compulsory detention in hospital under the Mental Health Act 1983, as amended by the Mental Health Act 2007.

ACTIVITY **2.4**

Which of the following matters potentially could come before a tribunal?

- *A student wishes to challenge a deportation decision.*

- *A parent disagrees with the allocation of school for their disabled child.*

- *A victim of crime is disappointed with the criminal injuries compensation award made to them.*

- *An independent adoption agency has had their registration cancelled.*

- *A single parent recently arrived in the UK has been refused council tax benefit.*

- *A transsexual person wishes to gain legal recognition of the gender in which they live.*

- *An ex-serviceman is keen to pursue a previously rejected claim for a war pension.*

- *A social worker has been removed from the social care register after a period of mental illness.*

Go to **www.justice.gov.uk/about/hmcts/tribunals.htm** *to check your answers.*

The Council on Tribunals, established in 1959, aimed to ensure that tribunals:

- Were accessible to all.

- Were quick, informal and as cheap as possible.

- Provided the right to an oral hearing in public.

- Gave reasons for their decisions.

- Were seen to be independent, impartial and fair to all.

While these principles remain relevant, Sir Andrew Leggatt's 2001 review of the tribunals system advocated a more enabling approach in which tribunals seek to ensure that applicants understand the procedures and feel that they have been fully heard. As a result, the Tribunals, Courts and Enforcement Act 2007 established a new statutory framework incorporating an Administrative Justice and Tribunals Council.

One of the main objects of the 2007 Act was to address concerns about consistency in decision-making, thought to be exacerbated by the variety of types of tribunal and number of people who sat as tribunal members. However, it is difficult to understand why the new terminology was adopted, since it is unlikely easily to be understood by the very people that tribunals seek to serve. Most of the previously existing tribunals have been incorporated into the new system but those which have other functions, such as Employment Tribunals and Agricultural Land Tribunals, continue to lead a separate existence.

There are two levels of Tribunal, First-tier and Upper. While the Upper Tribunal hears appeals from the First-tier Tribunal, it is also the first level of Tribunal in some types of case. Each Tribunal is divided into Chambers, which bring together areas of work requiring similar expertise.

The First-tier Tribunal has five Chambers:

- **Social Entitlement** – covering claims for financial benefits.

- **Health, Education and Social Care** – responsible for care standards, mental health, special educational needs and disability.

- **War Pensions and Armed Forces** – concerned with compensation in the context of military service.

- **General Regulatory** – covers a rather miscellaneous area, including consumer credit, estate agents and gambling.

- **Immigration and Asylum**.

The Upper Tribunal has four Chambers:

- **Administrative Appeals**.

- **Tax and Chancery**.

- **Lands**.

- **Immigration and Asylum**.

The Immigration and Asylum Chamber hears appeals from the similarly named Chamber of the First-tier Tribunal. Most other First-tier Chamber appeals are heard by the Administrative Appeals Chamber of the Upper Tribunal. It is only possible to appeal on a point of law, and permission must first be obtained either from the First-tier Tribunal or from the Upper Tribunal. There is a similar right of appeal from the Upper Tribunal to the Court of Appeal.

Each Tribunal Chamber is headed by one or two Chamber Presidents, over whom is the Senior President of Tribunals who is also a Court of Appeal judge. The Senior President has wide-ranging functions and must have regard to the need for:

- Tribunals to be accessible.

- Proceedings to be fair and handled quickly and efficiently.

- Members to be experts in the subject-matter of, or the law to be applied in, cases which they decide.

- Continuing development of innovative methods of resolving disputes that are of a type that may be brought before tribunals.

Tribunal decisions, for example that a sum of money be paid to an aggrieved party, can be enforced as if they were a court order to pay.

Most tribunals comprise three members, chaired by a legally qualified judge. There are more than 5,000 judicial office-holders within the tribunal system, a third of whom are female and around 10% of whom are from a minority ethnic group. The other members are usually a person with relevant professional expertise, such as a psychiatrist for the First-tier Tribunal (Mental Health), and a third person, often referred to as a lay member but who usually has some relevant knowledge or experience. Judges and members are not expected to undertake work outside their area of expertise and some tribunals make use of assessors to give expert opinion or advice in specialist areas.

Although some of the areas in which tribunals operate are quite complex, publicly funded legal assistance is only available for hearings before the First-tier Tribunal (Mental Health) and the Immigration and Asylum Chamber of the First-tier Tribunal (and even that is under threat). Consequently many applicants are unrepresented, or rely on organisations such as the Citizens' Advice Bureau or special-interest advocacy groups to advise or represent them, which places a heavy burden on what are often small organisations with many demands on their resources.

> *I really don't think any tribunal is suitable for a layman like me. My solicitor did all the talking and I did not speak at all because it was way over my head.*
>
> (Applicant to Social Security and Child Support Appeals Tribunal)

As tribunal hearings, like court hearings, are essentially adversarial rather than inquisitorial, tribunal judges often have to intervene in order to assist unrepresented applicants, achieve a fairer balance, or seek to avoid damaging confrontation. The Administrative Justice and Tribunals Council is considering whether there is scope for developing alternative dispute-resolution techniques to reduce the number (and, of course, the cost) of full tribunal hearings.

RESEARCH SUMMARY

Research into the experience of applicants to Employment Tribunals (Aston et al., 2006) found that claimants considered that the process should be more informal and less heavily reliant on legal terms and knowledge. Many felt inadequately prepared for their hearing, some had difficulty in following their case at all, and those without legal representation felt at a disadvantage. The research also found that a sympathetic attitude and active involvement on the part of the Chairperson was central to the quality of claimants' level of satisfaction.

A customer survey undertaken by the Tribunals Service found that 65% of tribunal applicants were satisfied with their overall experience. Unsurprisingly, satisfaction was closely linked to the outcome of the case, with applicants most likely to be successful being those who were represented at the hearing or who attended in person. Some dissatisfied applicants perceived that they were not treated fairly or sensitively, or that the tribunal was not impartial.

(www.tribunals.gov.uk/tribunals/Documents/publications/r7442)

Where do tribunals take place?

Some tribunals with a high volume of business, such as Employment Tribunals, regularly sit in designated premises, and hearings of the First-tier Tribunal (Mental Health) are held in the hospital in which the applicant is being compulsorily detained. Although most hearings are relatively informal, some are conducted more like a court, especially if there are opposing sides, which tends to be reflected in the layout of the rooms used.

Social circumstances reports for the First-tier Tribunal (Mental Health)

PRACTITIONER REFLECTION **2.2**

Former President of Mental Health Review Tribunals

I have seen many social workers at hearings. Most only seem to want to tell me what is not available for a patient if discharged. The one or two who stick in my mind are those who were both realistic and proactive in seeking to facilitate the release of a patient who needed supervision, but not continued detention.

Social circumstances reports have a key role in the decision-making process in the First-tier Tribunal (Mental Health) and advice on what should be included is contained in Section E of the Practice Direction First-tier Tribunal Health Education and Social Care Chamber Mental Health Cases issued in 2008. The Department of Health has also produced guidance notes and these in combination mean that social workers have to balance the need to meet the identified requirements with the provision of a good level of analysis and professional opinion, which is usually what the tribunal wants to hear (see Chapter 7).

Panels and inquiries

This description covers a range of investigative hearings which take place outside the court system in response either to apparent procedural failures, or to unresolved complaints. Except in the case of the first type of inquiry listed, and the second stage of the fourth, inquiries have no legal powers and depend on the co-operation of those asked to take part.

Types of inquiry

- Those ordered by a minister, such as that set up under the chairmanship of Lord Laming to examine the actions of the agencies involved in the life of Victoria Climbié. They are conducted like court hearings, are often held in public and have the power to enforce the attendance of witnesses and the disclosure of information. The social work team manager who refused to appear at the Laming inquiry was ultimately convicted of a criminal offence. Witnesses can be cross-examined on their evidence, as in a court, and the parties are often legally represented.

- Inquiries set up by a local authority, usually chaired independently and held in private. Their remit depends on the nature of the inquiry and the resources made available for it.

- Inquiries or reviews which involve one or more agency, such as those initiated by Local Safeguarding Children Boards.

- Complaints against local authorities, which are handled in two stages. The first takes place internally and, if the issue remains unresolved, an independent review panel can be asked to investigate. If this does not produce a resolution, the final arbiter is the local government ombudsman.

The future

The court system in England and Wales is not very logical, and is largely the product of the historical developments outlined in Chapter 1. The high financial and personal costs of litigation are driving the move towards more imaginative forms of dispute resolution, particularly in relation to civil and family law. Economic, regulatory, competitive and political forces have shaped the following challenges facing the legal profession (Legal Services Board, 2010, page 16):

- Improve access to legal aid services in the context of reductions in eligibility, fee rates and resources.
- Develop technologies to drive costs down.
- Promote affordable legal services for potential customers who are too rich for legal aid and too poor for mainstream services.
- Rebuild consumer trust.

Other moves to reduce costs include proposals to close a substantial number of magistrates' courts and reduce the number of crown and county courts, which will cause inconvenience to those who need to use them.

There are numerous books on the English legal system.

Partington, M (2010) *Introduction to the English legal system* (5th edition). Oxford: Oxford University Press.

A more academic, but still accessible, general text which explains the principal features of courts, the legal profession and the law.

Slapper, G (2011) *How the law works: A friendly guide* (2nd edition). London: Routledge.

This book has plenty of anecdotes to interest the general reader.

www.cafcass.gov.uk

Children and Family Court Advisory and Support Service. Its annual report gives an overview of changes within the family court system and examples of innovative practice.

www.cps.gov.uk

The Crown Prosecution Service has guidance about court processes for witnesses and victims, including explanatory material for young people.

www.justice.gov.uk

The HMCTS website has a wide range of information for users of courts and tribunals.

www.judiciary.gov.uk

A website which aims to make the judiciary more accessible.

www.magistrates-association.org.uk

Includes an interactive youth site.

www.ajtc.gov.uk

The Administrative Justice and Tribunals Council publishes regular newsletters.

Chapter 3
Legal language and decision-making

This chapter will help you to meet the following National Occupational Standards for social work.

- Key role 1: Prepare for, and work with individuals, families, carers, groups and communities to assess their needs and circumstances.
  - Work with individuals, families, carers, groups and communities to identify, gather, analyse and understand information.
- Key role 6: Demonstrate professional competence in social work practice.
  - Review and update your own knowledge of legal, policy and procedural frameworks.

Introduction

> Over nine out of ten cases heard by the Court of Appeal or the House of Lords either turn upon, or involve, the meaning of words.
>
> (Lord Hailsham, former Lord Chancellor, Hamlyn Lecture, 1983)

Lawyers thrive on words, as anyone who has ever read a legal document or communicated with lawyers will testify. Like most professionals, lawyers are also attracted to jargon and an additional barrier to communication in legal contexts is that Latin, Norman French and other historical expressions are still used, together with complex vocabulary and sentence construction. However, efforts are being made to introduce more accessible language into legislation and many Latin expressions have been replaced, so as to make them more easily understood by non-lawyers. In this chapter we try to demystify the most commonly encountered legal expressions and concepts, so that you can better understand what is going on. We also consider the process of legal decision-making, including what makes a good judge, deciding the facts and applying the law, assessing witnesses and the burden of proof.

Types of law

Civil law

Confusingly, this expression has different meanings depending upon the context. It usually means the law which applies to citizens when dealing between themselves, rather than that which regulates the behaviour of members of society, which is the criminal law. However, sometimes civil law is used in distinction from common law, which we explained in Chapter 1. The concept of civil law is derived in theory from Roman law, which means that the laws are written down in codes as, for example, in France. In broad terms, common law countries are England and Wales, Ireland, Commonwealth countries, and the United States of America. Civil law countries are Scotland, all European countries, and most other countries, apart from those listed above. Perhaps surprisingly, most Islamic countries are civil law countries with codes of law, and do not depend primarily on Shariah law, based on the Koran.

Common law

We have seen common law contrasted with civil law, and we have explained its meaning in other contexts in Chapter 1.

Criminal law

This is the law which every citizen must obey. Although it is possible for private individuals to prosecute people for breaching the criminal law, its main feature is that it is society, in the form of the state, which seeks to ensure that the criminal law is obeyed and that those who break it are punished. Today most prosecutions are undertaken by the Crown Prosecution Service. However, in the crown court the name of the case against an accused person is always *R v.,* in which *R* represents Latin for *Regina,* meaning Queen, or *Rex,* meaning King; *v.,* which appears in the titles of all legal cases, means *versus,* which is Latin for *against*. The Queen prosecutes people in the crown court on behalf of society because historically it was the Crown's role to protect citizens against criminals.

Sources of law

Common law and equity

We have already explained that one of the meanings of common law is the law which has developed as a result of decisions of judges, and that the rules of equity developed to supplement the common law. One of the remedies which equity invented was the injunction.

Precedent

A precedent is a decision in a case in which legal reasoning has been established. Precedent without an *a* describes the system by which judges must take account of previous decisions where relevant legal reasoning has been decided. First, they have to decide whether there is a relevant precedent that should be applied to the case. If so, and the decision is from a court higher than the court hearing the case, it must be followed. Judges are not bound to follow decisions from lower courts, or those on the same level, but may do so.

Statute

This is law which has been passed by Parliament, either by means of Acts or Statutory Instruments, which are made by government ministers subject to approval by Parliament. Statutory Instruments are usually designated *Regulations* or *Rules* or an *Order* and are identified by a number and the year in which they were passed. European Union laws applicable to England and Wales are either Regulations or Directives, again identified by a number and the year in which they were passed. Only Regulations have direct effect as soon as they have been made. Directives require our Parliament to legislate to bring into effect the relevant European Union law.

To clarify the concepts of common law, equity and statute, it may be helpful to illustrate them with reference to aspects of criminal and civil law:

* The criminal offences of murder, conspiracy and incitement to commit a crime are all contrary to *common law*. No Acts have been passed which identify them as offences, although there is legislation relating to them, such as the penalty to be applied when a person is convicted of murder.

* In contrast, the criminal offences of theft, forgery and assault are all contrary to *statute,* in that legislation specifically defines them as offences. As society has become more complex, most criminal offences are now subject to statute, although many were originally common law offences.

* Many civil causes of action, including breach of contract, trespass, negligence and debt arise at *common law*. However, the rules which determine what constitutes negligence have been established in past court judgements, starting with the case of *Donoghue v. Stevenson*, which you were asked to research in Chapter 1.

* Civil disputes about wills involve *equity.*

* An example of a civil cause of action arising from *statute* is divorce. As we saw in Chapter 1, when the foundations of our legal system were laid, marriage was for life and so after it was decided that there should be a means by which marriages could be dissolved, Parliament passed legislation which defined the grounds on which it could be permitted.

Figure 3.1 *Common law, equity and statute*

Public and private law

In suggesting that public law and private law can be contrasted, many lawyers would not understand what you were talking about. For most lawyers, public law describes the work undertaken in the Administrative Court of the High Court – judicial review. So, again confusion can result from using the same expression in different senses. The expression *public law*, in contrast to *private law*, is relevant to family law proceedings under the Children Act 1989, in that public law applications are those in which a local authority is taking action to protect a child and private law applications involve disputes between private individuals, usually the parents.

Powers and duties

This distinction is clear and important. Powers and duties both arise under statutes. Other sources of law do not impose powers and duties in the sense that the two concepts are contrasted. At common law, however, there is an important duty to take reasonable care not to cause damage, and failure to perform this duty is negligence. If a statute imposes a duty upon a person or organisation, it is an absolute requirement to do it. However, if a statute gives a power to a person or organisation, they may do it, but do not have to. In many cases involving local authorities, courts have said that they cannot simply choose to ignore powers, but must actively consider whether to exercise them or not.

Whether a statutory provision amounts to a power or a duty should be clear. Although lawyers are trained to interpret Acts of Parliament, all Acts are intended to be understood by people who might need to read them, if necessary with the help of the increasingly detailed explanatory notes which accompany them. If an Act states that *it shall be the duty* to do something, or the word *must* is used, the provision is likely to be a duty. On the other hand, if the Act uses the word *may*, it is almost certainly a power. It can be tricky, however, if the word *shall* is used, without it being stated that it *shall be a duty*. Depending upon the context, the problem with *shall* is whether the word is mandatory, which means that it must be done, or directory, which means that it ought to be done, but it may not matter too much if it isn't.

ACTIVITY 3.1

Consult a copy of any legislation or policy guidance applicable to your workplace.

- *Do you think that the provisions contained within it are powers or duties?*

- *If it is unclear, what might be the possible consequences for the service provider, employee or service user?*

You may find that even if the distinction between powers and duties is clear, other aspects of legislation, guidance or policy documents are less easy to interpret. For example, what will happen if a duty is not carried out? Who decides, and on what basis, whether powers are to be exercised? What redress is available to those affected by such decisions? This may go some way towards explaining why lawyers seem to be so focused on the meaning of words.

Negligence

Negligence in law just means carelessness. If you drive your car into another because you are not concentrating, you have caused damage as a result of your carelessness – your negligence. A duty to be careful is more likely to exist if the potential consequence of carelessness is that a person may be harmed or property damaged, rather than that someone loses money. This does not mean that you cannot ever be found legally liable for carelessness if you have not caused any harm or damage, but it is unlikely. Essentially, to be found to have been careless when someone has lost only money as a consequence, you must have given advice to that person and failed to take care in the advice which you gave. It is not careless to be wrong, it is only wrong to be careless. As long as any advice which you give is that which any reasonably competent social worker would give, there should be no problem.

Barristers used to be immune from allegations of negligence, at least in relation to what they did in court, but they are now liable in the same way as any other professional, as are solicitors and solicitor advocates. Barristers in private practice and solicitors must all be insured against professional negligence claims.

Expressions you may hear in court

What people are called

Advocate A barrister or solicitor who presents a case in court. This is different from the advocate who may assist clients at a tribunal hearing or who may have a more formal role as, for example, a mental capacity advocate under the Mental Capacity Act 2005. The expression was not much used in a legal context until solicitors began to present cases in court.

Barrister We explained the role and types of barrister in Chapter 2.

Clerk Other than in magistrates' courts, court clerks are not legally qualified. In the High Court clerks are called *associates* and their duties include recording the times of court sittings, swearing in witnesses and preparing the formal order at the conclusion of the hearing. County courts do not have clerks in the formal sense and if anyone is in court along with the judge and usher, it is likely to be a court administrator.

Legal executive Someone who works for a solicitors' practice or legal department, but who is not a qualified solicitor. However, members of the Institute of Legal Executives are qualified, although at a lower level of expertise than solicitors. Only members of the Institute should be referred to as legal executives, but in practice terminology is lax.

McKenzie friend See Chapter 5.

My friend How a barrister who is appearing in a case against a solicitor refers to the solicitor in court. In court, lawyers traditionally do not refer to each other by name, either formally or informally.

My learned friend How a barrister refers to another barrister in court.

Paralegal The first paralegals were often law students on a gap year when it was said that their terms of payment was all the beer they could drink. However, the role has gradually developed to one in which they support solicitors throughout the conduct of a case, and the National Association of Paralegals is recognised as an awarding organisation by Ofqual, the regulator of qualifications in England.

Solicitor We explained the role of a solicitor in relation to court proceedings in Chapter 2.

Usher The person who makes sure everyone is in the right place at the right time, provides drinking water and, in some courts, swears in witnesses.

Hearings

Application Hearing, other than the trial, in which a party is seeking a court order, which could arise from anything connected with the preparation for trial.

Case management conference Hearing in a civil or family case at which arrangements for the trial are determined. In public law proceedings the key issues are identified and the timetable monitored by the court, given effect by means of a Case Management Order.

Directions hearing Technically an application, where the focus is on deciding what steps are needed to prepare the case for trial, such as exchanging documents and filing witness statements.

First appointment Follows the initiation of local authority court action in relation to a child or children and incorporates the court's directions for the handling of the case, including where the case will be heard, the appointment of experts and an outline timetable.

In chambers Hearing from which the public and press are excluded. The term is now usually only used in family cases. Any other hearings to which the press and public are not admitted are usually described as *in private*.

Issues resolution hearing At which the court seeks to clarify, and if possible narrow, the issues in dispute arising from a local authority care application.

Plea and case management hearing, or PCMH Crown court hearing at which the accused person must say whether they admit any of the charges against them and at which arrangements for the trial are determined.

Pre-trial review Hearing before trial at which a judge considers the state of preparation of the case and its readiness for trial.

Trial Hearing of either a criminal or civil case, at which all the evidence is heard and the legal argument about the issues takes place.

Other legal terms

Accused Person facing a criminal charge. The term *defendant* is also used.

Acknowledgement of service Formal step by which a party who is being sued in a civil action records that they have received the relevant documents and states whether they intend to admit, or dispute, the action.

Acquit Find an accused person in a criminal case not guilty.

Adjournment Temporary suspension of the hearing. This can be a break for lunch or at the end of the day after which the hearing will resume when the court next sits, or a longer break to enable some action to be taken.

Administration order County court order which directs a person to pay a specified amount into court in respect of outstanding debts.

Affidavit Written statement of evidence, confirmed on oath or by affirmation to be true, and sworn before someone with authority to administer it.

Affirmation Declaration by a witness with no religious beliefs, or beliefs that prevent them from taking the oath, that the evidence that they will give is true.

Alternative dispute resolution, or ADR Process of trying to resolve a dispute by negotiation and compromise. This is a generic term covering the variety of ways in which it can be done. See Chapter 2.

Annul Declare no longer valid.

Appellant Person who appeals.

Bail Release of a person from custody until their next court appearance, usually subject to conditions.

Bailiff County court officer empowered to serve documents and execute warrants.

Brief Written instructions to a barrister, usually prepared by a solicitor.

> *The term 'red tape' to describe bureaucracy originates from the historical practice of tying up official government documents with red ribbon; pink tape is still wrapped round barristers' instructions, or briefs, another example of legal tradition.*

Claim Proceedings issued in the county court or High Court.

Claim form Formal step by which a civil action is started. Previously known in the High Court as a writ.

Claimant Person issuing a claim. Previously known as plaintiff.

Conditional discharge Discharge of a convicted person without sentence on condition that they do not reoffend within a specified period.

Contempt of court Wilful disregard of the judicial process, which can be punished.

Convict Find an accused person in a criminal trial guilty. A person is still convicted if they admit a charge in court, or if they accept a caution which requires an admission of guilt.

Corroboration Evidence which confirms or supports that of a witness.

Court of Protection Exists under the Mental Capacity Act 2005 to make decisions in relation to the property, healthcare and personal welfare of adults, and occasionally children, who lack capacity to manage their own affairs. The court has the same powers, rights, privileges and authority as the High Court. It operates from a central registry but can sit anywhere in the country.

Cross-examination Questioning of a witness by an advocate for a party other than the one on whose behalf the witness has been called to give evidence. See Chapter 10.

Damages Money claimed, or awarded as compensation, for physical or material loss.

Defendant Accused person in a criminal trial or, in a civil case, the person against whom a claim form has been issued.

Disclosure Process of listing relevant documents in a civil case, with a view to showing other parties what documents you have. See Chapter 5.

Divisional Court In addition to having their own original jurisdiction, all three Divisions of the High Court can hear appeals from lower courts and tribunals. Some types of appeal are heard by a Divisional Court of, usually, two judges.

Evidence in chief Evidence which the party calling a witness wants the witness to give and which they are prepared to give. In civil and family cases it is given in writing, called a witness statement. In criminal cases it is given by answering questions put by the advocate for the party calling the witness.

Hearsay Evidence which was not perceived by the witness's own senses. Usually it is evidence which a witness cannot confirm is true, because it was told to them by someone else. See Chapter 9.

Immediate issue letter Notifies parents or carers of the local authority's decision to initiate care proceedings.

Indictable offence Criminal offence which must be tried in the crown, rather than magistrates', court.

Injunction Court order which prevents someone from doing something, or, exceptionally, requires someone to do something. Breach of an injunction is contempt of court.

Inspection Process of allowing a party to whom you have given disclosure to read the listed documents, which is usually done by providing photocopies. See Chapter 5.

Interim Pending a full order or final decision.

Letter before proceedings Means by which a local authority sets out for parents or carers the nature of the concerns which it has in relation to the welfare of their child or children. Receipt of the letter triggers eligibility for non-means and non-merits tested publicly funded legal advice and assistance for those with parental responsibility.

Litigant in person Someone who conducts their case in court without legal representation.

Mediation Seeking to settle a dispute by using a mediator to try to bring the parties to agreement.

Mitigation Reasons given on behalf of someone found guilty to excuse or explain the offence in an attempt to minimise the sentence imposed, or steps taken to reduce a loss which has been suffered.

Oath Verbal promise by a person with religious beliefs to tell the truth.

Official Receiver Civil servant whose function is to act as liquidator when a company is being wound up, or as trustee when someone is made bankrupt.

Official Solicitor Acts for people who, because they lack mental capacity and cannot manage their own affairs, are unable to represent themselves and no other suitable person or agency is able and willing to act.

Party Participant in a court action.

Practice direction Steps to be followed prior to legal action, with the aim of maximising the chances of a settlement.

Pre-proceedings meeting Follows the letter before proceedings and is intended to facilitate agreement on a care plan between a local authority and the parents or carers of a child about whom there are serious welfare concerns.

> *In the pre-proceedings phase local authorities should feel free to do whatever is necessary in social work terms to assist parents.*
>
> (P v. Nottingham City Council and the Official Solicitor [2008] EWCA Civ 462)

Public law outline Establishes the framework for management by the court of local authority care applications.

Re-examination Further questioning of a witness on behalf of the party for whom they were called to give evidence, after the conclusion of cross-examination.

Respondent Person against whom an application or an appeal is made.

Sine die Latin expression meaning *without a day*, used when an adjournment is agreed but no date for the resumed hearing is fixed.

Statement of truth Declaration at the end of a written statement of evidence that the contents are true.

Summing up Review of the evidence in a criminal trial and directions on the law by the judge before the jury considers its verdict.

Surety Undertaking to be liable for another person's default or non-attendance at court.

Suspended sentence Sentence which does not take effect unless a subsequent offence is committed within a specified period.

Ultra vires Acting in excess of authority, doing something which there is no power to do.

Witness statement See Evidence in chief.

Although the legal profession is gradually adapting its language, you will not always understand the meaning of what you read or hear and some words in common use may be understood differently in a legal context. If this happens, we strongly encourage you to ask for an explanation, since no one can take a full part in any process if they do not understand what is going on, and you may be the only person who can help interpret a legal procedure to someone who is directly involved in it. Needing to ask for clarification does not reflect on your competence and offers a timely reminder to the lawyers of the need to think more carefully about the language they use.

What makes a good judge?

> *We need to be intelligent, knowledgeable about the law, but more importantly perhaps, wise in the ways of the world, sensitive to others from different backgrounds to our own, fair, open-minded and balanced, independent in spirit, courageous to do what is right even when it will be unpopular – perhaps most of all when it will be unpopular – whether with politicians, the executive or the media.*
>
> (Lord Chief Justice, 2010, www.judiciary.gov.uk)

In the open competitions which are the means by which people hoping to be judges are selected, there is a formidable array of *competences* to be demonstrated, as in most professions. The fundamentals of a good judge are said to be:

- Sound knowledge of the law.
- The ability to make findings of fact which are likely to be sound.
- Experience of life.
- Common sense.

Magistrates are expected to demonstrate six key qualities:

- Good character.
- Understanding and communication.
- Social awareness.
- Maturity and sound temperament.
- Sound judgement.
- Commitment and reliability.

These requirements are reassuringly straightforward, if rather general, and easy to recognise as generic professional skills. However, we note that the list of qualities required by magistrates no longer includes those considered necessary at the time of the first edition of this book, namely intelligence, integrity, the capacity to act fairly, and common sense.

Judicial undertakings

Judges and magistrates take two oaths on appointment, the Oath of Allegiance and the Judicial Oath. The Oath of Allegiance for someone who is Christian or Jewish is:

I, [name], do swear by Almighty God that I will be faithful and bear true allegiance to Her Majesty Queen Elizabeth the Second, her heirs and successors, according to law. So help me God.

For other faiths a reference to the appropriate name by which God is known, or to the appropriate holy book, is substituted and those without religious belief may affirm.

The Judicial Oath is:

I, [name], do swear by Almighty God that I will well and truly serve our Sovereign Lady Queen Elizabeth the Second in the office of [whatever the judicial post is], and I will do right to all manner of people after the laws and usages of this realm, without fear or favour, affection or ill will. So help me God.

The important aspects of the Judicial Oath are, first, that right must be done, not in the abstract, but in accordance with the laws and usages of England and Wales. In other words, judges promise to apply the law. Secondly, the law must be applied independently, *without fear or favour, affection or ill will*. In some countries corruption is a fact of life, even corruption of judges, but fortunately it is nearly 200 years since there has been any suggestion of corruption on the part of a judge in England and Wales.

How judges make decisions

How judges approach decision-making seems to be an area which is particularly mysterious to non-lawyers and yet, as we show, it is really quite simple. It used to be thought that judges could make fair and just decisions because they were endowed with superior wisdom but, in common with many professions, judges today are more accountable and open to criticism than they have been in the past. It is not that they have lost the skills which they had previously; if anything, with appointment by open competition and compulsory in-service training, they should be better informed and better trained. However, like social workers, judges are targets for politicians and the popular Press, and being subject to public criticism is now a hazard of judicial life, especially for those involved in sentencing or judicial review cases. During 2009/10 the Office for Judicial Complaints received 1,571 complaints against individual judicial office-holders, an increase of 18% on the previous year.

It is not widely understood that courts do not have complete freedom to do justice, or what seems fair and right, and often their discretion is quite limited, particularly in relation to sentencing, which is subject to strict guidelines. Sometimes judges need to interpret statute law, but ultimately they have to apply it, whatever their personal views may be. Most of the principles of common law have been laid down for many years and as we have seen, judges below the level of the Supreme Court are bound to follow previous decisions of courts higher than the one in which they sit. This is called *the doctrine of precedent*, and failure to follow the law which is binding on the judge is a ground of appeal.

In order to apply the law you need to know it, or at least where to find it, which is essentially an academic skill. All judges have legal qualifications and magistrates are advised by their clerk. However, the law, like any theory, has to be applied to practice, which is a skill judges have developed during their previous experience in practice. A common feature of legal disputes, however, is that there is no agreement about the facts. This is not a problem for judges trying criminal cases in the crown court, because the jury decides on the facts and the judge tells them how to apply the law to the various permutations of facts. Any other judge, however, first has to determine the contested facts to which the law has to be applied. Deciding a case is a bit like doing Sudoku. You know what the rules of the game are (the law). If you apply them to which numbers are in which square (the facts of the case as the judge or magistrates find them to be), the answer should follow. However, sometimes, particularly in family cases, the answer is not clear-cut. What is required then is an assessment of what is most likely to be beneficial, or, occasionally, least likely to be harmful, which often is derived from experience and common sense. Even in cases where applying the law to the facts produces an obvious answer, judges and magistrates usually try to convey their decisions in a way which makes them more acceptable to, or at least less likely to cause long-term difficulties for, the unsuccessful party.

Deciding the law

In many cases the applicable law is not disputed and the disagreement is about the facts to which the law should be applied. Sometimes there is no disagreement about the facts and the debate is about what law should be applied to them. In other cases, there are disagreements about the facts and the law.

Some people imagine that legal disputes can be resolved by looking up the answer in a book. However, applying the law is not like valuing a second-hand car, when if you know its manufacturer, model, year and mileage, you can discover its value. The law is essentially a series of principles and legal decision-making involves assessing how the relevant principles should be applied to the facts of a particular case. A legal dispute is really a dispute about what legal principles should be applied in order to resolve it, which can come about in different ways. There may be a difference between principles deriving from different sources. For example, there may be principles established by the common law, but also a relevant Act of Parliament which has modified the common law principles. There may be a European Regulation which could have influenced the principles. In either type of case, first it has to be decided whether there is any conflict between the different sources of the law. If it is found that there is, the issue depends on which set of principles or modifications takes precedence over the others.

A fairly frequent source of dispute is where it is suggested that different courts have made conflicting decisions on the same point. Again, the judge's first task is to decide whether in fact there are conflicting decisions, which involves considering what principle was established in each of the relevant cases, known as the *ratio decidendi*, which is the legal reasoning underlying a decision. The argument about legal principles is then based on whether one case can be *distinguished* from another, on the grounds that the legal principles, and not just the facts, were different. For example, if it was decided in one case that the owner of a dangerous animal had an obligation to ensure that it did not attack people, and the animal in question was a tiger, it might be possible to argue that the same principles applied in another case where the animal concerned was a lion. Conversely, if it was decided that the tiger's owner had an obligation to keep it in a cage, that legal principle would not necessarily apply equally to the owner of a sheep.

Sometimes different judges make inconsistent decisions about the principles applicable to a particular type of case, in which case another judge at the same level is free to choose which one to follow. Alternatively the judge could decide to follow neither and make their own decision. However, in such circumstances it is likely that permission would be given to appeal, so that the matter could be decided authoritatively. More difficult is a case where it is said that a decision of one court has been overruled by a decision of a higher court. Usually the higher court says that it is overruling the decision of a lower court, if that is what it intended. But it can happen that, while giving a decision on one set of principles, a higher court lays down a new set of principles which are inconsistent with the principles contained in a different series of cases (called *a line of authority)*. The question of whether the higher court has by implication overruled the second line of authority will come, initially, to a judge sitting at first instance.

Hopefully we have shown that the resolution of many legal disputes is an intellectual exercise approached in accordance with established principles and that courts rarely have as much scope for imaginative innovation as many people believe.

Deciding the facts

If there is a dispute about both the facts and the applicable law, the facts have to be decided (*found*) before the law can be applied. How judges and magistrates decide disputed facts is often shrouded in mystery, which is not helped by the way they explain that they have accepted the evidence of one witness rather than another. If a judge says, *I prefer the evidence of A to that of B*, how has this decision been made?

We will try and dispel some of the mystery.

Evidence of witnesses of fact

The English system of justice attributes something approaching iconic status to witnesses of fact, especially in criminal proceedings, but in practice this is difficult to understand because there are so many obstacles to accurate recall. These include memory, perception, overload, timescales, judgement, rationalisation and difficulties in estimation, all of which are discussed in Chapter 6 in the context of maximising accuracy in recording. Courts must take these factors into account, in addition to the manner in which the evidence is presented, when forming assessments of witnesses offering evidence of fact.

Assessing truthfulness

How do courts decide when a witness is being untruthful? We are probably all accomplished liars at one level. Think of those unwanted gifts you have enthused over or how frankly you have answered questions about someone's appearance. This sort of social untruth is common and although you may think that there is a difference between little white lies and deliberate intention to deceive, both are told with the hope and expectation that they will be believed. Often it comes down to what different people are prepared to be untruthful about and how good they are at doing it. However, we also need to be aware of the temptation to rationalise remembered facts to fit a broad hypothesis or personal belief, which can lead to untruthfulness or inaccuracy, albeit often unconscious. So how do judges decide whether evidence is accurate or not?

Documentary evidence

Leaving aside the possibility of forgery, fortunately rarely encountered, documents produced at the time of the events in question usually provide the best representation of what actually happened. In cases with a significant amount of contemporaneous documentary material, courts are likely to accept as accurate evidence which matches the documents. However, the sooner after the event a record is made, the more accurate it is likely to be, which is why your case records are so important. If they are comprehensive, balanced, objective and compiled promptly, there is a good chance that a court will regard them as accurate accounts of the events concerned. Most business transactions are well-documented in correspondence and e-mails, and so in ordinary civil litigation there is usually a considerable amount of documentary material for the court to consider. In complex commercial litigation witnesses often do not have, and do not purport to have, any recollection of events, other than that prompted by the documents produced at the time, which is why in many commercial disputes there is no real argument about the facts.

Assessing witnesses of fact when there are no, or few, documents

Without the support of documents the process of assessing evidence potentially becomes more complicated. The likelihood of there being no, or few, documents is greatest in criminal cases when either the jury or magistrates must decide which facts to accept. Judges who have to choose between conflicting evidence of witnesses of fact, when there are no documents to assist, have a difficult task. The main advantage which they have over anyone else is experience. Factors such as consistency, grasp of detail, fairness, apparent willingness to assist and standing up to cross-examination will enhance a witness's credibility. There is obviously a risk that judges will get the assessment of witnesses wrong, but the system recognises that their assessment is as likely to be as accurate as anyone else's by making it almost impossible to appeal against judges' assessment of witnesses.

Expert evidence

When dealing with children, the court needs all the help it can get.

(Butler-Sloss, L J, in *Re M & R (Child Abuse: Evidence)* [1996] 2 FLR 195)

The court's task in assessing expert evidence is different from that of making an assessment of evidence of witnesses of fact. It is most unlikely that there will be any question of the expert being deliberately untruthful. Often experts do not give evidence of facts at all, although that will probably not be so in your case. However, judges frequently have to decide between different expert opinions, and the Court of Appeal has stated that they must give reasons for not accepting any expert evidence. Judges differ in how they approach the evidence of experts and much depends on how familiar they are with the particular area of expertise. As a result of practice in a particular field, for example family law, some judges become familiar with experts in that area and feel able to evaluate their evidence. But what about unfamiliar areas?

In some types of case, where the issue was essentially one of valuation, judges used to be expected to reach a decision midway between what opposing experts contended. However, now there is usually a single joint expert in such cases and so the need to split the difference has largely gone. In other cases, where compromise is not necessarily appropriate, judges therefore have to grapple with expert evidence and decide which opinions to accept. So how is this done? There are basically two methods:

- assessing qualifications, grasp of the subject and presentation;

- trying to get into the substance of the expertise.

Trying to understand an unfamiliar area of expertise, to a level which enables you to decide who is right and who is wrong, can seem daunting. However, most of us regularly do this in one way or another.

ACTIVITY 3.2

If two doctors, A and B, express different views about a personal medical matter, how would you decide which to accept? Which of the following factors would influence you most?

Continued

ACTIVITY 3.2 *continued*

- Dr A is older and has been in practice for longer than Dr B;

- Dr B holds postgraduate qualifications, which Dr A does not;

- Dr A has only worked the relevant specialism for a few months, while Dr B has two years' experience;

- Dr A is confident in his manner and seems to have a good grasp of the case, whereas Dr B seems rather hesitant and nervous;

- Dr B has provided some research findings to support his opinion;

- Dr A is more optimistic about the situation than Dr B;

- Dr B is inclined to use jargon, while Dr A is clear in his use of language;

- Dr B has considered several possible options, whereas Dr A only seems to have considered one course of action.

Now consider whether a judge is likely to approach it any differently from you.

The best way to be a helpful witness is to try to understand the task facing the court.

Essentially judges are likely to feel that any area of expertise should be capable of being explained to someone of reasonable intelligence who is prepared to make the effort to understand it, so that if the basis for an opinion cannot be explained with sufficient clarity for the judge to understand, they are likely to reject the opinion, however eminent the person putting it forward. Of course, while trying to understand why experts hold different views, it may become apparent that experience and qualifications are a factor. However, this is different from simply going with the more experienced, or better-qualified, expert without understanding what the issues are. Judges also need to avoid being swayed by competent presentation. We have all come across plausible presenters who rely on work which has been done by others or who, if challenged, cannot demonstrate essential elements of the expertise they claim to have.

Burden of proof

So far we have said nothing about burden of proof. This may surprise you, but in practice it is not as important as you might think. Of course, for a court to make a decision the evidence needs to cover everything necessary for a case to be made out, or a defence established. Proof beyond reasonable doubt, or proof which makes you feel completely sure, is really only required when juries or magistrates are trying criminal cases. If a key element is not covered by evidence, then there is no proof in respect of that element, and the case fails. The burden of proof is also theoretically important in a case where someone has been acquitted in a criminal court of an offence against a child, and the local authority is seeking a care order based on the same facts. Acquittal of a charge where the burden of proof is beyond reasonable doubt does not mean that a care order cannot be obtained in civil proceedings where the burden of proof is the balance of probabilities.

The different levels of proof are not very important in making many legal decisions, because of how evidence is presented. As we have seen, it is rare in civil or family cases that the only evidence is that of witnesses of fact. If there are contemporaneous documents which support the evidence, it is usually proved at least on a balance of probabilities, and probably beyond reasonable doubt. On the other hand, if there are no supporting documents, and the court is not satisfied that the factual evidence is accurate, the case for the party whose evidence has not been accepted fails. It would not be a case of accepting the evidence, but deciding that it did not make the threshold of a balance of probabilities; it would not be accepted at all. The only situation in which the burden of proof might be important is if the judge is thinking: *Well, this might be correct, but then again, it might not*, when the burden of proof can tip the balance.

ONLINE RESOURCES

www.hmcourts-service.gov.uk/infoabout/glossary/legal.htm

Contains a glossary of legal terms

Chapter 4

Values and principles in law and social work

This chapter will help you to meet the following National Occupational Standards for social work.

- Key role 5: Manage and be accountable, with supervision and support, for your own social work practice within your organisation.
  - Deal constructively with disagreements and conflict within relationships.
- Key role 6: Demonstrate professional competence in social work practice.
  - Identify and assess issues, dilemmas and conflicts that might affect your practice.
  - Devise strategies to deal with ethical issues, dilemmas and conflicts.

Introduction

There is a tendency for social workers to regard lawyers as superior, privileged and remote from real life and we acknowledge that some of them still seem to cultivate this image. However, in our experience it is much less common than it used to be. The legal profession, like any other, incorporates a wide range of skills, personal characteristics and beliefs in its practitioners and, like social work, has experienced significant changes in recent years. These include training costs and requirements, regulation and accountability, restrictions in the public funding of legal services, and media attention. One of the aims of this book is to demystify aspects of the law which create barriers for social workers doing court work, and key aspects of the interface between them are the values and principles which shape the two professions.

In this chapter we show that how lawyers are governed, and the principles which underpin their profession, are remarkably similar to those which apply to social work. There are issues which apply to lawyers, and not to social workers, because of the nature of their work, and there are matters which apply to solicitors, but not to barristers, because of their different roles. However, principles such as fairness, honesty, transparency, confidentiality, anti-discriminatory practice and commitment to social justice are as central to the law as they are to social work, and there have been recent examples of judges and lawyers resisting what they regard as attacks by politicians on the essential values of their profession.

Where there are perceived barriers between individual members of each profession, we suggest that in part these may stem from the contrasting skills and approaches which lawyers and social workers bring to communication and problem-solving. Differences in personal attributes and motivation towards their respective careers may also be factors in individual cases.

ACTIVITY 4.1

- *Without thinking too deeply, identify five words which you might use to describe lawyers.*

- *Next, identify five words to describe other professionals, such as teachers or doctors.*

- *Now assess whether the words you have chosen are generally positive, neutral, negative or a mixture of the three.*

- *What does this tell you about your preconceived ideas or stereotypical views of the legal profession?*

- *What descriptions do you think lawyers might apply to social workers?*

This exercise demonstrates that we all hold opinions about people whom we perceive as different from ourselves. Sometimes these attitudes stem from personal experience, but they may also be based on unchecked assumptions, inaccurate second-hand information or unconscious prejudices. It is only by acknowledging this possibility, and addressing the potential consequences, that we can begin to identify and seek ways of overcoming the barriers which impede effective professional relationships.

A statutory professional framework

Social workers

Until the Care Standards Act 2000, social work as a profession was not regulated by statute. There was no restriction on anyone describing themselves as a social worker and there was no statutory professional body to set and maintain standards, although some social workers voluntarily belonged to the British Association of Social Workers, which required them to adhere to its codes of practice. In general, therefore, the public, and service users in particular, had no guidance on what to expect from social workers and no means of redress if they were dissatisfied or poorly served. The General Social Care Council (GSCC) took on this role in 2003, but as it was beginning to get to grips with the task of professional regulation, the government decided to transfer its responsibilities to the Health Professions Council (HPC) from 2012. Many social workers are uneasy about an alliance with professions such as chiropody, podiatry and paramedical services, and are concerned that it may compromise social work's independence and value base. It is hard to imagine, for example, lawyers being regulated alongside probation or police officers.

Currently student social workers, unlike law students, must register with the professional body and abide by its codes of practice. The GSCC also makes enquiries about the health and criminal record of applicants for registration and requires verification and endorsement by an approved person. However, these requirements may be modified when the HPC assumes responsibility for social work. The majority of GSCC council members, who determine issues concerning professional standards, are laypeople rather than members of the social care profession, thought to be an important aspect of rigour in the context of regulation.

Barristers

In the Middle Ages most skilled workers belonged to a guild, which set standards and regulated its members. As we have seen, barristers' guilds were the Inns of Court until 1894, when the General Council of the Bar, generally known as the Bar Council, was established to determine questions of professional etiquette. The Bar Council also has a statutory role in relation to barristers as a result of the Legal Services Act 2007, which provides that a person only has a right to appear in a court, *a right of audience*, if they comply with the Act's requirements. Among other things, barristers must be educated and trained to approved standards, they must be members of a professional body with enforceable rules of conduct, and they must provide a proper professional service, which is similar to the requirements for other professions, including social work. Since 2006 barristers have been regulated, and standards of entry to the profession have been set, by the Bar Standards Board (BSB), which is independent of the Bar Council.

Solicitors

We are only concerned here with solicitors conducting litigation, not with other services they offer, such as conveyancing. The original purpose of the Law Society, founded in 1845, was to *promote professional improvement and facilitate the acquisition of legal knowledge* but it later evolved into providing regulation of solicitors. Because solicitors are more numerous than barristers and because they have more opportunity than barristers to commit misdeeds, due to their access to clients' money, Parliament passed laws affecting the conduct of solicitors rather earlier than in the case of barristers. The principal Act is the Solicitors Act 1974, although it has been altered considerably since it was first passed. Solicitors cannot practise unless they have been admitted as a solicitor, their name is on the roll of solicitors (that is, they have not been struck off), and they hold a practising certificate, which can have conditions attached. The cost of a practising certificate is much greater than that required by GSCC or HPC for registration. In 2007 the Law Society restructured and established a separate arm, the Solicitors Regulation Authority (SRA), which includes an independent Consumer Complaints Board. The SRA is now moving towards 'outcome-focused and risk-based regulation' which it asserts will better serve the interests of consumers.

The Bar Standards Board and the Solicitors' Regulation Authority both have minority lay membership, which represents a significant shift from the previous culture of self-regulation, albeit not as convincing as some users of legal services would like to see.

Professional standards

Like all professionals, lawyers take their professional standing seriously. For example, barristers do not handle clients' money, an important distinction between them and solicitors and one of the fundamental principles contained within the barristers' code of conduct. In addition to honesty and the duty to ensure that their conduct is not prejudicial to the administration of justice or likely to diminish public confidence in the legal profession, barristers operate under other strongly worded principles, which may partly explain the single-minded way in which they sometimes appear to approach their work:

303

A barrister:

a) must promote and protect fearlessly, and by all proper and lawful means, the lay client's best interests, and do so without regard to his own interests or to any consequences to himself or any other person (including any colleague, professional client or other intermediary or another barrister, the barrister's employer or any Recognised Body of which the barrister may be an owner or manager);

b) owes his primary duty as between the lay client and any other person to the lay client and must not permit any other person to limit his discretion as to how the interests of the lay client can best be served;

307

A barrister must not:

a) permit his absolute independence, integrity and freedom from external pressures to be compromised;

b) do anything (for example, accept a present) in such circumstances as may lead to any inference that his independence may be compromised;

c) compromise his professional standards in order to please his client, the court or a third party, including any mediator.

Although these principles, of which we only provide an extract, are similar to those of social work, there is an edge to the language which makes them, if anything, more demanding than those of social work, which tend to use less specific and more qualified expressions, such as *seek to ensure* and *as far as possible* rather than *must/must not*. However, in addition to owing duties to their clients, employed social workers are usually accountable to a range of stakeholders, which can present them with conflicts and ethical dilemmas which sometimes lawyers may fail to appreciate.

Barristers' professional standards are mirrored by solicitors' rules, of which there is a huge number covering a wide range of issues. The most fundamental are contained in the Solicitors' Code of Conduct 2007, the most basic of which is Rule 1, in which again the client's needs are central:

You must act with integrity (1.02);

You must not allow your integrity to be compromised (1.03);

You must act in the best interests of each client (1.04);

You must provide a good standard of service to your clients (1.05).

Solicitor-advocates are also bound by the Law Society's code of advocacy, which mostly reproduces the principles of the code of conduct of the Bar.

ACTIVITY **4.2**

In relation to professional standards, if you were a client, would you regard the following behaviours as more serious, or more likely, in a social worker or a lawyer?

- *Spending more time on cases they find rewarding.*
- *Offering unrealistic assurances.*
- *Sharing personal experiences.*
- *Not preparing adequately for decision-making meetings.*
- *Being influenced by people they perceive as more powerful.*
- *Avoiding clients they find difficult.*
- *Ignoring clients' wishes and instructions.*
- *Giving advice beyond the limits of their expertise.*
- *Not keeping the client fully informed.*
- *Blaming policies, procedures, or lack of resources for any shortfall in services.*

In encouraging you to think about clients' expectations of lawyers and social workers, and the pressures and priorities of each profession, this exercise will help you recognise similarities and differences in the ways in which lawyers and social workers approach and manage their work.

Confidentiality

Confidentiality is so fundamental to how lawyers operate that you have to look quite hard in their codes of conduct to find any reference to it. Without confidentiality, the administration of justice could not work. Barristers and solicitors are bound to keep confidential the affairs of their clients but, as with social workers, this confidentiality is not absolute and in limited circumstances it is permissible, or even required, for lawyers to divulge information obtained in confidence. The most obvious examples are where disclosure is required by law, such as in cases involving money laundering, drug trafficking or terrorism, when lawyers must also comply with any order to produce documents required by the police under the Police and Criminal Evidence Act 1984.

Lawyers also have a duty to the court to assist in the administration of justice and not to deceive or mislead. So, if a court requires a lawyer to disclose confidential information, they must comply. This is rare, but it could happen, for example in order to discover the whereabouts of a child.

More difficult is the situation in which a lawyer, while not being required to, may wish to disclose information from a client which relates to the safety of another person. If someone tells their lawyer that they intend to commit a crime, such as kidnap a child, the law treats the information as not being confidential and so it can be disclosed. If there is no suggestion of a potential crime, the lawyer's position is difficult. In principle, information provided by clients should be kept confidential. However, professionals can disclose confidential information in exceptional circumstances.

CASE STUDY 4.1

W v. Edgell [1990] 1 All ER 835

After shooting several people, W was detained in a secure psychiatric hospital. Subsequently he applied to a tribunal to be discharged, and while his responsible medical officer supported the application, it was opposed by the Secretary of State. W's solicitors asked Dr Edgell, a consultant psychiatrist, to prepare a report to support W's application for release. However, he concluded that W had a psychopathic disorder which, combined with a long-standing interest in firearms and explosives, made him a continuing risk to the public. After Dr Edgell's report was received by his solicitors, W withdrew his application and the report would not normally have been disclosed to anyone else. When Dr Edgell discovered this, he sent a copy to the hospital, which passed it to the Secretary of State, who sent it to the tribunal. W then sued Dr Edgell for breach of confidence, but his claim failed on the ground that the public interest in disclosing Dr Edgell's professional opinion was greater than the public interest in maintaining W's confidentiality.

In this case it was a question of balance, which is why it is difficult to say how great the public interest in disclosure needs to be in order to override the principle of confidentiality. However, it would need to be a very significant interest to override the confidentiality which is fundamental between lawyers and clients.

In the case of other professionals, the position is less clear. An ordinary employee, with no particular duties of confidentiality other than not to disclose their employer's private business, is free to reveal any significant breach of the law by their employer. However, most professionals, including social workers, operate on the basis that confidentiality is integral to their work and professional rules or codes of practice generally support this principle. Therefore, failure to maintain confidentiality could expose a professional to disciplinary action by their employer or professional body. No disciplinary tribunal would criticise a professional who was required by a court to disclose confidential information and, as in the Edgell case, courts always aim to balance the public interest in knowing the information with the interest of the professional's client in keeping it private. However, historically courts have tended to require that non-legal professionals disclose confidential information if it is considered that there is a valid reason for wanting it. There is, however, an exception in relation to information which non-lawyers obtain in the course of trying to negotiate the settlement of a dispute. Discussions in these circumstances are treated by the law as *without prejudice*, which means that everything is privileged, no matter who was involved and whatever the outcome, even if the person concerned interfered in the dispute without being asked. For example, as long as he is acting as a conciliator, confidential information received by a probation officer is privileged and does not have to be revealed to the court (see Chapter 5).

Conflict of interest

It probably goes without saying that barristers and solicitors are not permitted to become involved in conflicts of interest. Two types of conflict are contemplated by the barristers' code of conduct:

- They must not accept instructions if, as a result, they would be professionally embarrassed, which includes lacking sufficient experience or competence to handle the case, or not having the time to prepare it properly. We are sure that social workers would welcome a similar professional rule. A connection with someone, such as a client or a court, which makes it difficult to remain or be seen to be objective, or a risk of conflict between two or more clients, or of confidential information being leaked between clients, are also included.

- As barristers are usually instructed by solicitors, there is a particular problem if a barrister decides that the instructing solicitor has been negligent in advice given to the client or in the conduct of the case. However, it could also be a less extreme situation in which there is no suggestion of negligence, but the barrister thinks that the client would be better off instructing another solicitor. If a barrister considers that there is a conflict between the client and the instructing solicitor, he must tell the client to go elsewhere. There is a specific rule about this because any barrister who does this is unlikely to receive any more work from the solicitor in question, which would otherwise be a powerful incentive to keep quiet.

The solicitors' rule against conflict of interest is more straightforward. There is a duty not to act if the solicitor, or his practice, owes separate duties to two or more clients in relation to the same matter, or if the duty to the client conflicts with the solicitor's own interests. However, solicitors can act for two or more clients in the same matter if they have a common interest in it and all the parties agree. This might happen, for example, in a child care case where a solicitor could act for both parents.

ACTIVITY **4.3**

Identify some potential conflicts of interest that a social worker may encounter (for example, receiving a referral which relates to a family personally known to you) and assess how far your professional codes of practice help to guide or protect you in these situations.

This exercise encourages you to consider further the common ground and differences between lawyers and social workers, particularly in relation to the level of protection or support each can expect from their professional organisations and codes of practice.

Principle of being non-judgemental

This principle is fundamental to social work; however, in view of the fact that *judging* people is a central task of courts, how can it ever be said that lawyers are non-judgemental? Over the years, stories have circulated to illustrate the sort of professional dilemmas which lawyers can face:

CASE STUDY 4.2

A barrister successfully defended a man against a charge of burglary, in which it was alleged that he had stolen a valuable gold watch. After he was acquitted, he leant over the dock towards his barrister, saying in a loud stage whisper, 'So, what shall I do with the watch?'

Another story concerned a man who, having been acquitted of stealing antique jewellery, sent his solicitor a letter of thanks enclosing a gift of Victorian silver cufflinks.

These rather unlikely stories nevertheless raise an issue which is sometimes put to lawyers on social occasions: how can they defend someone they know to be guilty or present a case they know, or suspect, to be false? The answer is likely to be similar to that which social workers might give if asked how they could work with people who had neglected or abused children, in that they would normally seek to distinguish between respecting the person and condoning their behaviour. Lawyers' professional duty is to do their best for their client, which involves giving the best advice and trying to achieve the best outcome for them in any legal proceedings. It does not matter whether lawyers believe their clients or not, but it is their responsibility to advise on the risks of a court not accepting what they say. If a client persists in presenting a particular account, despite being advised of the possible consequences, the lawyer's duty is to put forward their case, without deceiving or misleading the court (see under Fairness below). However, if someone tells their lawyer that they are guilty, but nevertheless intend to fight their case to the bitter end, or that the evidence they intend to give is untrue, the lawyer would be unable to act for them.

The principles which underpin this approach are:

- Lawyers should not judge their clients and must proceed on the basis that what they say is true, however unlikely it may seem.

- Even people who are dishonest or guilty of crimes have the right to legal advice and representation.

- The rules of English criminal law allow technical points to be used for the benefit of defendants which could result in a guilty person being acquitted. Lawyers who take advantage of technical points on their client's behalf are simply carrying out their professional duty by following the rules.

However, like all professionals, lawyers and social workers are expected to use their knowledge, skills and values in order to make professional judgements which stand up to scrutiny in court.

Fairness

An aspect which concerns many people when dealing with lawyers is how they treat you in court, particularly when cross-examining you. You should be reassured that it is not open season on witnesses for barristers or solicitor advocates, and their rules clearly state what they can or cannot do. In particular each:

- *Must not make statements or ask questions which are merely scandalous, or intended or calculated only to vilify, insult or annoy either a witness or some other person.*

- *Must if possible avoid the naming in open court of third parties whose character would thereby be impugned.*

- *Must not by assertion in a speech impugn a witness whom he has had an opportunity to cross-examine unless in cross-examination he has given the witness an opportunity to answer the allegation.*

- *Must not suggest that a victim, witness or other person is guilty of crime, fraud or misconduct, or make any defamatory aspersion on the conduct of any other person, or attribute to another person the crime or conduct of which his lay client is accused unless such allegations go to a matter in issue (including the credibility of the witness) which is material to the lay client's case and appear to him to be supported by reasonable grounds.*

(CCB Rule 708; The Law Society's Code of Advocacy Rule 7.1)

This means that you should only be cross-examined on the facts of the case, your credibility or your competence. You should not be criticised, unless it is relevant to the case and you have been given an opportunity to respond to any criticism.

There are other aspects of fairness which are important in the context of understanding what happens in court. Barristers are not permitted to put forward an argument in court unless they consider that it is properly arguable. They cannot, therefore, just put forward any argument suggested by their client. Barristers and solicitor advocates must bring to the court's attention all relevant decisions, including those which do not support their client's case, and if something goes wrong or there is an irregularity, they cannot keep it quiet in the hope of an appeal, but must bring it to the court's attention. They also must not make up the evidence.

More generally, solicitors must not behave deceitfully or so as to take an unfair advantage of anyone. Therefore, you ought to be able to have confidence in their frankness and honesty. Once in court, you are unlikely to have contact with solicitors for an opposing party, because they are not supposed to interview anyone who has retained their own solicitor, which, as a social worker involved in court proceedings, is likely to include you. In dealing with legal representatives for opposing parties, solicitors have a duty to behave with frankness and good faith, consistent with their duty to their clients. While solicitors may not feel able to disclose confidential information concerning their client, they certainly must not mislead.

The issue of fairness in relation to social workers is explored in more detail in Chapter 7. However, those who have contributed to this book have emphasised its importance in court settings.

> *Clients get very upset if facts are not presented fairly, even if they relate to something which seems quite unimportant. Once that happens, mistrust develops, which extends into more important areas and is very difficult to overcome.*

> (Independent advocate)

Anti-discriminatory practice

The strongest framework of anti-discriminatory practice relates to barristers who must not discriminate directly or indirectly on grounds of race, colour, ethnic or national origin, nationality, citizenship, sex, sexual orientation, marital status, disability, age, religion or political persuasion. Rather oddly, the relevant rule in relation to solicitors differs only in that it has no reference to political persuasion, but it is clear that the rules of both professions demonstrate a strong commitment to the promotion and maintenance of equality.

Some of the most revealing evidence as to the differing professional pressures on, and public expectations of, lawyers and social workers is found in the types of complaint referred to their respective professional bodies.

Social workers
- Professional competence.
- Abuse or violence.
- Improper use of IT equipment.
- Criminal convictions.
- Harassment or discrimination.
- Inappropriate relationships with service users.   (GSCC, 2008)

Solicitors
- Professional competence.
- Breach of solicitors' accounts rules.
- Failure to comply with professional requirements (supervision, payment of counsels' fees, solicitors' indemnity rules, business code).
- Improper use, or misappropriation, of clients' money.
- Criminal convictions.
- Delay in dealing with cases.   (SRA, 2010)

Barristers
- Professional competence.
- Rudeness or misbehaviour in or out of court.
- Failure to comply with CPD requirements.
- Misleading a court.
- Failure to follow instructions.
- Fee dispute.   (BSB, 2009)

Figure 4.1 *Types of complaint in order of frequency (most frequent first)*

Partnership and self-determination

From the start of their training, social workers are encouraged to see partnership with clients as the foundation of ethical practice, which is one reason why they feel uneasy in legal settings where rules can appear to take precedence over clients' wishes and feelings. Lawyers' relationships with their clients start by receiving instructions. They then advise them and, whether or not the advice is accepted, seek to obtain the result closest to what their client wants, which reflects the principle of self-determination and is a form of partnership. However, the partnership is subject to market forces in that if the client is dissatisfied they can usually go elsewhere. For social workers, partnership and self-determination have additional dimensions, involving a delicate balancing act between maximising choice and independence for their clients, exercising legal powers and duties, managing risk and taking account of available resources. Additionally and significantly, social workers have to work with involuntary clients which lawyers, for the most part, do not.

RESEARCH SUMMARY

Freeman and Hunt (1998) identified the qualities which make a 'good' solicitor in the eyes of parents seeking representation in care proceedings:

- *Being partisan and committed enough to put up a good fight.*

- *Showing a personal interest.*

- *Appearing caring and understanding.*

- *Being willing to listen.*

- *Being prepared to believe their client/s.*

- *Involving parents in discussions, negotiations and decision-making.*

- *Being able to advise, inform and explain in simple, direct and honest terms.*

Lack of continuity was the factor they most disliked.

How lawyers approach problems

In order to work effectively in legal settings, it is not necessary for you to learn to think like a lawyer. However, you do need to engage with the complexity of the law-practice interface (Cull and Roche, 2001), which is easier if you understand how lawyers think.

Lawyers are trained to interpret the law and apply it to solve legal problems. As we have seen, their first involvement in a case is likely to involve being asked for advice. In order to be able to consider what legal principles may apply in any situation, they must assemble, and evaluate, material which shows the facts or what a court, if the matter is contentious, might find the facts to be. They should know what types of fact are potentially relevant to their advice and, as we have seen, they do not need to be satisfied that everything they are told by their client is true. However, they need to see all relevant documents and any other evidence which supports the client's case, so that they can assess how a court might decide it if there is a challenge and advise accordingly. Once the client's version of events has been established it is possible to apply the law to it, which involves considering the applicable statutes or regulations and any relevant cases which have been decided previously. It is the focus on the law, rather than any other approach to the facts, which distinguishes the lawyer's approach from that of a non-lawyer.

CASE STUDY **4.3**

Birmingham City Council v H (No. 3) [1994] 2 WLR 31

This case involved a baby with a 15-year-old mother, who was herself looked after by the local authority and had complex needs. A social worker would regard them both as equally entitled to services but the legal approach was different. The House of Lords put the welfare of the baby as being paramount above that of the mother, because the court was dealing with an application concerning the baby, not the mother.

This example illustrates the fact that whatever non-lawyers might think are the ethical rights or wrongs of a case, or whatever they consider would be a desirable result, lawyers are concerned primarily with what the client's instructions are and what, if any, legal duties and powers are applicable to a particular situation. Once a case comes to court, rather than objectively to seek justice or establish the truth, the lawyer's aim is to obtain the most satisfactory outcome for their client, consistent with their professional rules and duty to the court, which involves deciding, with their client, how best to present the case without misleading the court. We explore in Chapter 8 the relevance of court rules, but in many instances it is possible to compare the lawyer's preparation of a case with establishing a game plan. For example, if a potential witness is known to be frail and likely to become confused, it might be decided not to call them to give evidence, to avoid risking the case being harmed by the witness creating a poor impression. Court hearings are, of course, not a game in the normal sense, but they are about making decisions in accordance with the law, which could be said to represent the rules of a game. Whoever wins is decided by applying the rules to the circumstances of the case. The only mechanism which exists for finding out what really happened in any situation is a public inquiry, which is rarely established.

Motivation and personal attributes

When considering the nature of the relationship between social workers and lawyers, it is worth reflecting on your motivation for taking up a social work career and why social work appeals to you. You may have been influenced by personal experience of adversity; you may feel that you can identify with people who are socially disadvantaged or excluded; you may hope that working with people will bring particular challenges and rewards; you may have been told that you are a good listener or you may have enjoyed helping and supporting people in the past. If you ask lawyers why they chose the legal profession, many will offer very different reasons, such as an interest in researching and applying academic aspects of the law, an attraction to the drama, or even glamour, of the courtroom, or the possibility of earning a reasonable amount of money. However, some lawyers whose remuneration is primarily publicly funded, as in criminal law, would dispute the realism of the latter ambition and increasingly people are regarding a legal career, particularly as a solicitor, as an opportunity to make a difference in social contexts such as those involving domestic violence, immigration or human rights. Nevertheless, the contrast between some of these motivating factors suggests how tensions may develop between members of the two professions when they are approaching the same situation from a different standpoint.

Assertiveness

I don't think I've ever met a lawyer who didn't appear supremely confident.

(Expert witness)

Most of the lawyers you meet professionally will be experienced and comfortable in court, which requires high levels of assertiveness and professional confidence. Observing a court is a good way of identifying the practical skills required of lawyers when practising advocacy. However, for social workers such perceived levels of confidence can sit uneasily with their training and commitment to identify and minimise power differentials and barriers between themselves and service users.

A central aim of this book is to help you feel more confident in the court setting. Confidence involves feeling more in control and approaching difficult situations without being overwhelmed by anxiety or self-doubt. Although assertiveness is not traditionally thought of as an essential social work skill, it involves (McBride, 1998):

- Behaving in a way which is neither aggressive nor passive.

- Feeling, and looking, confident about yourself.

- Respecting yourself and others equally.

- Having clear goals.

- Being able to say you don't know or don't understand.

- Speaking out for yourself or others.

- Making your opinion heard in a way which takes account of others' feelings.

- Listening to alternative points of view, even if you disagree.

- Having the widest possible range of behaviour options at your disposal.

All of these attitudes or skills accord with basic social work principles, in that they stem from valuing yourself and others, and they are particularly valuable in the court setting. They can be developed throughout your career by continually assessing your strengths, evaluating your practice and identifying areas for potential development.

ACTIVITY **4.4**

Think of a time when you have been assertive.

- *What did you want to achieve?*

- *How did you feel immediately beforehand?*

- *How did you feel at the time?*

- *What specific behaviours did you employ?*

- *How did you feel afterwards?*

- *How can you use this experience productively in the future?*

This activity encourages you to reflect on and evaluate your thoughts and behaviour so as to identify your strengths and future learning needs. Taking control of your development in this way is itself empowering and will establish a good foundation for gaining confidence and skills to support you in court work.

Once you have begun to identify areas for development, there will always be opportunities for you to work on them, which do not require any special preparation on your part.

- Speaking out at meetings.

- Saying 'no' to unreasonable requests.

- Asking for clarification when you do not understand.

- Systematically prioritising your work.

- Taking action to reduce stress, rather than suppressing it.

- Seeking out those whom you find difficult to deal with, with a view to establishing more effective communication.

- Regarding feedback as an opportunity rather than a threat.

- Using observation to identify role models.

JRTHER
EADING

Beckett, C and Maynard, A (2005) *Values and ethics in social work.* London: Sage.

This text includes some relevant exercises and comparative analysis of the professional standards and regulation of social work and law.

McBride, P (1998) *The assertive social worker.* Aldershot: Arena.

Contains lots of activities designed to develop assertiveness.

www.barcouncil.org.uk Bar Council

www.barstandardsboard.org.uk Bar Standards Board

www.gscc.org.uk General Social Care Council

www.hpc-uk.org.uk Health Professions Council

www.lawsociety.org.uk Law Society

www.sra.org.uk Solicitors' Regulation Authority

Part 2
Preparing for court

Chapter 5
Legal advice and representation

This chapter will help you to meet the following National Occupational Standards for social work.

- Key role 1: Prepare for, and work with individuals, families, carers, groups and communities to assess their needs and circumstances.
  - Inform individuals, families, carers, groups and communities about your own, and the organisation's duties and responsibilities.
  - Assess needs, risks and options, taking into account legal and other requirements.

Introduction

In this chapter we explore the public funding of legal costs and possible alternative ways of obtaining advice and representation, including advocacy and McKenzie friends. We also consider factors which are relevant to obtaining legal advice in a professional capacity, including pre-hearing consultations, disclosure and inspection of documents, without prejudice communications, legal professional privilege and public interest immunity. We explore the relationship between social workers, lawyers and other professionals, including children's guardians, and discuss the need to ensure suitable preparation and support for service users.

Public funding of legal costs

The administration of the publicly funded system of legal aid is undertaken by the Legal Services Commission, which describes its vision as *to make sure clients can access the help they need to address their legal problems*. The Commission is responsible for establishing, maintaining and developing two separate services: the Community Legal Service, which provides legal aid in civil cases, insofar as legal aid is available in those cases at all, and the Criminal Defence Service, which helps people who are under police investigation or facing criminal charges. However, the costs of such services are under increasing pressure: in 1998 over half the population was entitled to legal aid but now less than a third meets the eligibility criteria (Legal Services Board, 2010, page 16).

Civil cases

Public funding for ordinary civil litigation has almost disappeared and is only available in limited circumstances to people whose financial resources do not exceed prescribed levels. The financial limits differ according to the type of legal assistance sought, and the eligibility calculation is complicated. Generally, financial limits are low and the Legal Services Commission Funding Code sets out the criteria used to determine whether to provide funding. As different criteria are set for different types of case, it is essential to consult the most recent edition.

The Code recognises five levels of service:

- Legal help, covering an initial meeting and follow-up advice.

- Family mediation.

- Family help (lower), which covers more substantial advice, assistance and negotiation.

- Family help (higher), if it is found necessary to issue proceedings.

- Representation at court.

What this means is that the government has limited the funding available for civil legal aid, and applies restrictive criteria in deciding how to allocate that money, even if the applicant satisfies the financial eligibility criteria.

Family cases

In family cases legal aid is currently available for children, and those who have parental responsibility for them, who are subject to proceedings under the Children Act 1989 ss.31, 43, 44 or 45. In order to receive public funding solicitors must be on the Law Society's Children Panel, which has branches covering solicitors approved to represent children, adults and local authorities respectively in public law family proceedings. In other types of family case the usual civil legal aid rules apply, except that conditional fee agreements (see below) are not permitted, so that the potential obstacle to the grant of legal aid that it might be possible to enter into a conditional fee agreement does not apply. A large part of the Community Legal Service's budget is committed to family cases, which limits the funds available for other civil cases.

Criminal cases

Anyone who is detained at a police station is entitled to receive independent free legal advice, which does not depend on assessed ability to pay and is provided by solicitors under contract to the Criminal Defence Service. Advice and assistance with criminal cases before charges have been made is available to people in receipt of some state allowances, including Income Support and income-related Employment and Support Allowance, and those whose income and savings are below a certain level.

Legal representation following criminal charges is offered at three levels:

- Representation order, covering representation at court by a solicitor and, if necessary, a barrister. This is means-tested.

- Advocacy assistance, applicable only to people in prison.

- Advice and representation by the duty solicitor at a magistrates' court in relation to a limited range of minor offences.

The time taken by the means-testing process has led to concerns that people are being left unrepresented in court, even in situations where a prison sentence is likely.

Changes to legal aid

As part of the overall review of public expenditure, the government is planning significant reductions in the costs of legal aid, saving around £350 million annually by 2015. To achieve this, large areas of work are likely to fall outside eligibility for public funding altogether. These could include immigration, clinical negligence, debt where homes are not immediately at risk, non-violent domestic disputes and child contact. You should check the up-to-date position via an appropriate website. However, it is clear that the consequences of such changes will impact on growing numbers of people who need legal advice or assistance, giving greater relevance and prominence to alternative ways of obtaining legal help and an increase in the number of people acting on their own behalf (*litigants in person*).

Alternatives to public funding

If civil legal aid is not available, apart from paying for legal advice and representation privately, receiving assistance under some household insurance policies, or obtaining help from a trade union or professional association, the principal options are:

Conditional fee agreement

This is an arrangement whereby legal advisers do not charge a fee unless the claim in question is successful. They are not permitted in criminal or family proceedings. This is fine as far as it goes, but in most civil litigation the losing party must pay the successful party's costs. Under a conditional fee agreement, therefore, an unsuccessful party is still liable to pay the other party's costs, whereas a legally-aided losing party only has to pay costs to the extent that his means allow.

Post-event legal expenses insurance

This is insurance against legal costs obtained in return for a premium, which tends to be high. The terms of such insurance vary.

Conditional fee agreements and post-event legal expenses insurance both amount to gambling on the outcome of litigation. It is true that this is the seasoned bet of the regular punter rather than the traditional flutter on the Grand National, because lawyers willing to consider a conditional fee agreement first assess the merits of the case, as do post-event legal expenses insurers. However, there is always an element of risk as the outcome of litigation is rarely guaranteed. Many lawyers will not operate on a conditional fee basis, because they are sufficiently in demand not to have to run the risks of doing work for which they may not be paid.

Pro bono arrangements

One of the fundamental principles of the legal profession is that legal advice and assistance should be available to everyone who needs it, which has prompted some lawyers to accept work on a *pro bono* basis. *Pro bono* is short for *pro bono publico*, meaning *for the good of the public*. The theory is that as it is in the public interest that legal advice and assistance be given, the work is not charged for. However, as it is voluntary work it is down to individual lawyers whether they are prepared to accept cases on this basis. The principle that barristers are obliged to act for any client who wishes to engage them is subject to the exception that they do not have to take on work for nothing.

Fixed fee interview

Some solicitors offer a time-limited interview, either free or for a fixed fee regardless of income, which can be useful if you want to know whether you have a case worth defending or pursuing and how much it is likely to cost.

Law centres

Law centres are community-based organisations, answerable to local committees, which offer legal advice and representation in the general area of social welfare law, including housing, debt, employment, discrimination, immigration and welfare benefits, but not usually family work. Although they operate on the same basis as private solicitors' practices, they are non-profit making and receive funding from central and local government, trusts and charities. As a result, they may be able to help clients who are ineligible for public funding. The distribution of law centres is patchy and they tend to operate in inner-city areas.

Citizens' Advice Bureau

This well-known registered charity, with over 3,000 branches, *helps people resolve their legal, money and other problems by providing free information and advice and by influencing policy makers,* primarily through trained volunteers. In 2009 the organisation helped nearly two million people with over six million enquiries, the most common of which related to debt, state allowances, employment, housing and legal problems.

McKenzie friends

Adults have an absolute right in any legal proceedings to represent themselves if they wish, or, as is becoming more common, they cannot afford to pay for legal representation themselves. However, only qualified and properly instructed lawyers can represent someone else, whether or not they are related to them, so a parent cannot represent their adult child, for example. Nevertheless, it is recognised that someone acting on their own behalf may need some help.

In *Collier v. Hicks [1831] 2 B & Ad 663 at 669* Lord Tenterden CJ said:

> *Any person, whether he be a professional man or not, may attend as a friend of either party, may take notes, may quietly make suggestions and give advice; but no one can demand to take part in the proceedings as an advocate, contrary to regulations of the court as settled by the discretion of the justices.*

No one appears to have taken advantage of the potential opportunity this offered until 1971 when, in a divorce case, *McKenzie v. McKenzie* heard by the Court of Appeal, it was decided that the trial judge was wrong to have prevented one of the parties, who was acting in person, from having assistance of the type envisaged by Lord Tenterden. Following this decision, the name of the case involved has been attached to the role of someone who helps a litigant in person, now known as a *McKenzie friend*.

Courts decide whether to allow a litigant to be assisted by a McKenzie friend, who is in theory permitted to undertake only a limited range of tasks. However, in practice a competent and reasonable McKenzie friend can be of great help to both the litigant and the court, who may allow a McKenzie friend to speak in court, even if it is not strictly within the limits of their role. Due to the restrictions in civil legal aid, the prominence of McKenzie friends has increased significantly, resulting in a number of Court of Appeal decisions about the nature and extent of their involvement.

CASE STUDY **5.1**

Re H (McKenzie Friend: Pre-Trial Determination) [2002] 1 FLR 39

A father successfully appealed against a judge's ruling that he could not have a McKenzie friend at a contact hearing being held in private.

Re O (Children) (Hearing in Private: Assistance) [2005] 3 WLR 1191

The Court of Appeal linked a litigant's right to have a McKenzie friend with the right to a fair trial contained in Article 6 of the European Convention on Human Rights. As a result there is a strong presumption in favour of a court granting permission for an unrepresented litigant to be assisted by a McKenzie friend.

So important have McKenzie friends become in family cases that in 2008 the President of the Family Division issued guidance on what they may or may not do.

A McKenzie friend can:

- Provide moral support for the litigant.

- Take notes.

- Help with case papers.

- Quietly give advice on points of law or procedure, issues that the litigant may wish to raise in court and questions the litigant may wish to ask witnesses.

A McKenzie friend must not:

- Act on behalf of a litigant in person.

- Address the court, or examine any witnesses.

- Act as the litigant's agent in relation to the proceedings.

- Manage the litigant's case outside court, for example by signing court documents.

Figure 5.1 McKenzie Friends

Social workers can act as a McKenzie friend, which could be useful in tribunals where legal aid is only available in very restricted circumstances. However, a note of caution:

> *A risk you run in representing someone at a tribunal is that you usually get blamed if the outcome is not what the client wanted.*
>
> (Independent advocate for older people)

Advocates

> *We are not regarded as professionals ... people ignore you ... sometimes at court the social workers and lawyers do not even say 'good morning' ... it feels really abusive ... I often think that this must be how the client feels.*
>
> (Independent advocate for people with learning disabilities)

We have already seen that *advocate* is a generic term used to describe qualified lawyers who represent people in court. However, advocacy also describes services offered by individuals and organisations to people who need help in getting their views heard in relation to matters as diverse as housing, finance, relationships, employment, health and complaints. The Mental Capacity Act 2005 also provides for the appointment of independent mental capacity advocates to represent the interests of people who lack capacity in relation to certain personal welfare decisions.

The settings in which advocates operate include courts, tribunals, panels and less formal decision-making areas such as case conferences and reviews. Advocacy services tend to be specific to a particular client group and may be wholly or partly user-led, often combining the advocacy role with that of an information resource or pressure group. Although training varies, many advocates have built up considerable expertise in helping people handle legal problems and communicate in legal settings. Bateman (2000, page 47) describes the principles of this kind of advocacy, which are similar to those applicable to other professional activities.

- Act in the client's best interests.

- Act in accordance with the client's wishes and instructions.

- Keep the client properly informed.

- Carry out instructions with diligence and competence.

- Act impartially and offer frank, independent advice.

- Maintain confidentiality.

Despite the expansion of advocacy services, many professionals are still ignorant or wary of their involvement and it can be an isolated role. However, it is important to appreciate the potential benefits of advocacy, both because it can support people who cannot easily express their own views, and also because advocacy skills are at the heart of much of the legal and procedural framework of social work practice.

Stages of advocacy

Bateman (2000, page 140) summarises the six stages of advocacy.

- Presentation of the problem.

- Information gathering, which requires good interviewing skills.

- Legal research.

- Interpretation and feedback to the client.

- Active negotiation and advocacy, which require assertiveness, good communication and negotiation skills.

- Litigation, which is usually the last resort.

The next activity will help you to develop a structured approach to problems, incorporating these principles.

ACTIVITY **5.1**

Think of a situation in which you were involved in the interpretation or application of rules or procedures, or the presentation of someone else's views.

- *Can you identify Bateman's stages within your own actions?*

- *If any stages were omitted, could this have affected the final outcome?*

- *How did you evidence the principles of advocacy?*

- *What changes would you make if faced with a similar situation in the future?*

Advocacy often simply involves making those responsible for decision-making aware of the facts of a case, so that the rules can be fairly applied. However, even this apparently straightforward process can be very time-consuming as, for example, in housing disputes, where the regulations are increasingly complex.

- *To practise the information-gathering and research stages of advocacy, when you are involved in a situation relating to rules, procedures or regulations, start by compiling a chronology of the facts.*

- *Next, match this to any available documentary evidence and the relevant rules as you understand, or have researched, them. This will enable you to prepare a diagrammatic representation of the arguments in support of the case (similar to the rationale of the skeleton argument described in Chapter 8).*

Court 37

Court 37 in the Queen's Bench Division of the High Court illustrates the way in which the law allows litigants in person to seek justice.

As we have seen, adults have the right to represent themselves in any court, and the Royal Courts of Justice has a branch of the Citizens' Advice Bureau to assist people who wish to start an action or make an application without legal representation. Court 37 is permanently designated for the hearing of what are said to be urgent applications; every day there is usually at least one litigant in person and there may be several, particularly on Fridays. It can take time for the judge to discover what the litigant's problems are and sometimes, if there is a particular grievance against the Queen, Prime Minister or other public figure, there is little the court can do. Not all litigants accept the limitations of the court's powers, which is why Court 37, a large Victorian court, where the judge is several feet higher and closer to the door than the litigant, is allocated for this purpose in place of a more open-plan court.

First steps in taking legal advice

> *Often the only thing that families involved in care proceedings have in common with the social workers is that they are all worried about going to court. If the social workers are too well-prepared, they won't even have that.*
>
> (Parents' Aid representative)

Usually you are involved in a court case because one of your service users is. Therefore, in addition to preparing yourself, you must consider the needs of your client and any others involved with the case, such as foster carers. People who are looking to you for support will be reassured if you understand what is likely to happen. Additionally your managers and legal advisers will be undertaking their own preparation and you will need to communicate with them about it.

When and why do you have to be prepared?

Sometimes it is necessary to respond to an emergency or take part in a process which has been started by someone else. However, you are most likely to be involved in legal proceedings because your employer, usually a local authority, has decided to initiate them.

If there is a choice, the obvious decision is not to start proceedings until you are ready, which is when legal advice has been taken and all the evidence necessary to support the case has been assembled.

In family cases involving children, there are timescales to which courts expect the parties to work. This is to comply with the requirements of the Children Act 1989 s.1(2) that *the court shall have regard to the general principle that any delay in determining the question is likely to prejudice the welfare of the child* and the Public Law Proceedings Guide to Case Management, usually referred to as the Public Law Outline (MoJ, 2010b), which is concerned with establishing a timetable and narrowing *(funnelling)* the issues at an early stage. However, the complexity of the decision-making involved makes it difficult to prepare properly and meet the deadlines, while at the same time maintaining the rest of your caseload.

> *You haven't got time to sit down and physically go through everything any more.*
>
> (Social worker quoted by Beckett et al., 2007)

RESEARCH SUMMARY

Jessiman et al.'s (2009) initial evaluation of the operation of the Public Law Outline (PLO) found:

- *Inconsistent and occasionally inflexible application of the PLO by the judiciary.*
- *Poor local authority compliance, particularly in relation to the filing of pre-proceedings documents.*
- *A need to improve timings of disclosure of data from other agencies and professionals.*
- *Inadequate welfare input at initial stages in some areas due to delays in appointing children's guardians.*

Timely supervision provides the opportunity to think through the professional dilemmas and personal challenges which may arise, and your manager's support is essential to ensure that planning, decision-making and recording is thorough, and everyone is kept fully informed.

CASE STUDY 5.2

In the course of care proceedings, the magistrate asked the social worker what she thought would be the impact on the child of separation from the parents, and the social worker replied, 'None'. Afterwards, the children's guardian and expert witness asked the social worker whether this was really what she believed and she replied, 'Well, I was put on the spot and I couldn't think what to say'.

With the support of good supervision and preparation, the social worker might have anticipated this kind of question and been able to give an informed response. As it was, she let herself down, did nothing for the reputation of her profession, and, most importantly, overlooked the interests of the child. We suggest that, as soon as court proceedings appear likely, you draw up a personal timetable, incorporating all the deadlines of which you are aware and a realistic assessment of the time required to prepare and update statements, attend meetings and hearings, receive supervision and undertake all the necessary investigation, reading and checking.

It is unlikely that you will seek legal advice directly yourself, but you should ensure that your managers know when you feel that a case may be moving towards the threshold for legal proceedings. Often a legal planning meeting is initiated by a decision made in another multidisciplinary forum such as a case conference or review. Your employers are likely to have a legal section with lawyers experienced in dealing with the sort of cases which your department is likely to produce and they can also consult outside lawyers for more specialist advice. If legal advice is sought at a relatively early stage, before it is urgently necessary, it can be considered in a calmer atmosphere and assessed, jointly with lawyers, in relation to the evidence which exists, who can provide it and whether it supports a case being brought, which is likely to involve liaison with other agencies. Similarly, if you are supporting someone facing a criminal charge or other court action, it is important to know where to obtain advice before the date fixed for any hearing.

Confidentiality

Although confidentiality is a core social work principle, your duty of confidentiality towards service users and others is overridden once legal advice is sought. In other words, you should not normally hold back information from legal advisers on the grounds that you owe a duty of confidentiality towards your service users or someone else. As we have seen, lawyers have a clear duty of confidentiality towards their clients, so you should feel confident that anything you say to them about a service user's affairs, or any doubts or concerns you express, will not go further.

Legal representation

In addition to taking pre-proceedings legal advice, the parties involved will need to be represented at any hearing. If it is decided to instruct a barrister (counsel), there will almost certainly be a solicitor from the local authority's legal department, or from an outside firm, involved. The solicitor will need access to the case file and will want to meet you. A statement from you will almost certainly be necessary. This is unlikely to be the statement which eventually is put before the court as your evidence, but it is the best way in which to tell the lawyers about the issues in the case. Although you can be guided as to what needs to be covered in your statement, you must write it yourself. Take notice of any advice about what should be included, or any language which the solicitor suggests is unclear, but otherwise be careful. Be very, very cautious about making significant changes or agreeing to omit something which you think should be included, as there is a considerable risk of you being criticised if you do. The solicitor is unlikely to be criticised because it is your statement, not theirs (see Chapter 7).

If a barrister has been brought in (*instructed*), you will probably attend a meeting with them, called a *conference* when it is with a junior barrister, or a *consultation* when it is with a QC. Usually conferences or consultations take place in the barrister's chambers which, if you work near London, are likely to be in London. Depending upon the complexity of the case, you may have to attend a number of such meetings.

There are two principal purposes of a conference or a consultation:

- To enable the barrister to obtain information about the case from those with first-hand knowledge.

- To give legal advice.

It is likely that those who attend will include people who know about the facts of the case and others who are responsible for decisions about how matters should proceed in the light of the advice given. It is not the barrister's responsibility to make investigations into the facts of a case, or to collect evidence for use in court. Barristers therefore do not normally interview witnesses in order to discover what evidence they would give at a trial. Consequently barristers need to meet those with factual knowledge of the case so that they have full knowledge of the facts on which their advice is being sought.

Once legal representation has been arranged, the lawyers must be kept up-to-date with developments in the case so that they can give further advice, or reconsider advice given. Again, you might not make contact directly with lawyers, and some employers restrict this to contain costs, but you should ensure that your manager knows of any significant developments.

Disclosure and inspection of documents

Ordinary civil cases

In ordinary civil litigation, other than in family cases, each party must show the other parties any documents which are relevant to the dispute, because documents which existed at the time events occurred usually shed considerable light on what actually happened. This has been the case for many years and is not a recent development arising from open government or freedom of information. You can safely leave to the lawyers the question of what needs to be disclosed, but it is useful to know what is involved in the process and the important exceptions. A document means anything in which information is recorded and includes electronic records, tape recordings, photographs, films, e-mails, text messages and voicemails.

A party shows other parties its documents in two stages:

- A list of them is provided, known as *disclosure*.

- Other parties are permitted to see the documents which have been disclosed, called *inspection*.

Which documents have to be disclosed?

In ordinary civil litigation all the documents on which the party making disclosure relies in support of its own case and any which adversely affect its case, or the case of another party, must be disclosed. Each party is likely to have the documents on which it is relying, or at least copies of them, but it may no longer have other types of document which it should disclose. You do not avoid the need to disclose documents just because you no longer have them. However, you are only required to make a reasonable search for any on which you yourself do not intend to rely. If several copies of a document exist, such as a memorandum copied to several people, it is not necessary to disclose each copy, but any copy which contains modification, obliteration or other marking is treated as a separate document.

There are exceptions to the obligation to show documents to other parties, in which case, although they must still be listed in the disclosure statement, they do not have to be offered for inspection. Obviously you do not need to show a document which you no longer have. Also, documents do not need to be disclosed if public interest immunity, legal professional privilege, litigation privilege or without prejudice rules apply (see below). Solicitors used to send their trainees to look at other parties' documents, which sometimes revealed interesting material on the reverse. Now it is usual to provide photocopies or electronic copies, but anything on the reverse of the original must be included. The duty of disclosure continues throughout the proceedings, which means that any relevant document which was missed the first time and later turns up must be disclosed.

What use can be made of documents disclosed in the course of litigation?

Fortunately, rights to make use of them are restricted. A party to whom documents have been disclosed can only use them for the purposes of the proceedings in which the disclosure took place, unless the document has been read to or by the court, or referred to at a public hearing, or the court gives permission for another use of the document, or the party who disclosed it and the party to whom it belongs agree to it being used for another purpose. Even if a document has been read to or by the court, or referred to at a public hearing, the court may still restrict or prohibit its use.

Making a false disclosure statement is contempt of court.

Family cases

In family cases there is no obligation to give general disclosure of the type described in other civil cases. Instead, if disclosure is necessary for the fair disposal of the proceedings, a party can be ordered to give disclosure of specific documents. However, in all cases involving children, the parties and their lawyers have a duty to make frank disclosure of all relevant information and the Bar Council has produced guidance for barristers who may need advice about the nature and extent of their professional obligations when the question arises of whether or not to disclose material unfavourable to their clients' case (www. barcouncil.org.uk/guidance/professionalpracticecommitteeguidanceondisclosureofun helpfulmaterialdisclosedtocounselinfamilyproceedings).

Criminal cases

The basic rule in criminal cases is that the prosecution must disclose all relevant documents to the defence. In crown courts, and in some types of cases heard by magistrates, the defence must disclose the nature of the defence but not the evidence relied on to support it. There are separate procedures for the seizure of documents by the police to use as evidence with which we need not be concerned. However, the first two exceptions to the general rule of disclosure in ordinary civil cases covered below also apply to protect documents from seizure by the police, so that documents which are covered by public interest immunity or legal professional privilege should not be seized.

Public interest immunity

One of the grounds on which a party can withhold a document which otherwise should be disclosed is if public interest immunity applies. This principle applies in cases where breach of confidentiality in a document will cause harm to the public interest which is greater than any harm caused by non-disclosure, illustrated by the following case.

CASE STUDY **5.3**

D v. National Society for the Prevention of Cruelty to Children [1978] AC 171

The NSPCC received a report that a child was being ill-treated. Following investigation, it was decided that the allegation was unfounded and the child's mother wanted to know who had made it, so that she could sue the person concerned. The NSPCC refused to say and the House of Lords decided that NSPCC records were covered by public interest immunity, because the NSPCC's work depended on people being confident that they could report cases without their identity being revealed.

Public interest immunity can also cover social work case records and applies in criminal cases as well as in civil and family cases. However, documents which are protected by public interest immunity do not have to be kept confidential. Any document which is referred to by a witness must be disclosed and consequently, in most cases in which you are involved, your case records are likely to be disclosed as part of the evidence. In child care cases the presumption is against a local authority relying upon public interest immunity. Children's guardians always have a right to see local authority records.

Legal professional privilege

It is a fundamental legal principle that people should be able to consult lawyers freely and frankly, confident that what they have said will not be passed on to anyone else without their consent. A Victorian judge, Sir George Jessel, explained why this principle is needed:

> *The object and meaning of the rule is this: that as, by reason of the complexity and difficulty of our law, litigation can only be properly conducted by professional men, it is absolutely necessary that a man, in order to prosecute his rights or to defend himself*

from an improper claim, should have recourse to the assistance of professional lawyers, and it being so absolutely necessary, it is equally necessary, to use a vulgar phrase, that he should be able to make a clean breast of it to the gentleman whom he consults with a view to the prosecution of his claim, or the substantiating his defence against the claim of others; that he should be able to place unrestricted and unbounded confidence in the professional agent, and that the communications he so makes to him should be kept secret, unless with his consent ... that he should be enabled properly to conclude his litigation.

(Anderson v. Bank of British Columbia [1876] 2 ChD 644)

The courts have recognised that the administration of justice is impossible without legal professional privilege and so no one else is ever entitled to know what legal advice has been sought or given about anything. It applies to all legal advice, not just in the context of litigation, so advice received before there is any question of litigation is also privileged. Obviously in many organisations legal advice may have to be shared among several people. The privilege is not lost by doing that, even if a non-lawyer summarises to another person what the lawyer has said. However, subject to the possibility that such a document may be covered by public interest immunity, ordinary communications between staff of a social work agency, or between one department and another, are not privileged unless they relate to the giving or receiving of legal advice.

Litigation privilege

While legal advice is always privileged, an additional type of privilege applies only in relation to preparing a case for a hearing, called litigation privilege. This concerns documents which have been produced principally in order to give or receive advice or to collect evidence in connection with actual or anticipated litigation. The privilege therefore covers witness statements and experts' reports in ordinary civil litigation until it is decided to provide copies of the documents to the other parties. Consequently, in ordinary civil litigation, drafts of witness statements and experts' reports are covered by litigation privilege. It also covers requests for evidence, for example by letter, and responses to such requests. However, in children's cases, there is no litigation privilege in relation to experts' reports. This is to promote the non-adversarial nature of such proceedings and also because the court's consent is required to disclose documents to the expert, or to have the child examined.

CASE STUDY 5.4

Re L (a minor) (police investigation), [1997] AC 16

Parents, who were addicted to heroin, obtained permission to show court papers to a chemical pathologist, hoping to demonstrate that their child could have ingested methadone accidentally. The pathologist, however, did not support this contention and his report had to be disclosed to the court concerned with the child's welfare, against the wishes of the parents.

In criminal cases defendants can always rely on litigation privilege. However, the prosecution must disclose any material assembled in anticipation of the trial which it decides not to use. This is called *unused material.*

Without prejudice communications

In civil and family cases the law aims to promote settlement of disputes to avoid expensive and potentially damaging trials. Consequently, documents produced with a view to negotiating a settlement are privileged from disclosure if settlement is not achieved. Of course, the parties to the negotiations will each have copies of the documents, so the principle is really about none of them being able to refer in court to what was said during the negotiations. Subject to limited exceptions, the negotiations cannot even be referred to if there is a settlement. For many years lawyers have headed letters about negotiations *'without prejudice'*, but this formula does not have to be used. Documents which are part of negotiations aimed at achieving a settlement are privileged whether or not the words *'without prejudice'* are included. On the other hand, using those words does not make a document privileged if it is not a part of negotiation aimed at a settlement. Sometimes people include the words *'without prejudice'* hoping that what is written will not be held against them. This is not the proper purpose of the privilege and such documents are not protected from being put in evidence in court.

CASE STUDY 5.5

Nathan, 18, who is supported by a local authority leaving and after-care team, lives in a privately rented bedsit. One evening he has a party at which his friend gets drunk and breaks a plate glass door. Nathan refuses to pay for the damage as it was not his fault. However, the landlord threatens to sue him for the repair costs and Nathan fears that he will lose his accommodation. He wants to make an offer to the landlord in the hope of settling the matter before it gets to court. However, he is worried that by doing this, he will be admitting responsibility and will be liable for the whole amount, plus any court costs. Nathan can be reassured that such an offer would be privileged and would not have to be disclosed in the course of any subsequent proceedings if it was rejected. Of course, the landlord may not be willing to negotiate, but legal action is never risk-free for any party and this example demonstrates that knowing the rules might be helpful in particular circumstances.

Relationships with lawyers

A potential area of tension is the precise nature of the relationship between you and the lawyers representing you, or more usually your employer, as it is they who will pay the bill. In most lawyer/client relationships, the client gives instructions, considers the advice offered, and decides how to proceed in the light of this advice. However, it can sometimes be unclear who exactly is the client (you, your line manager, a service manager or your employer as a whole, who might also be the lawyer's employer), and although it depends on the personalities and experience of those involved, you may need to clarify your position and the decision-making process in your agency at the outset.

RESEARCH SUMMARY

Dickens (2005, 2006) explored how local authority social workers, their managers and lawyers worked together in family cases. He found that generally inter-professional relationships worked well, but that tensions were never far from the surface. The strongest criticisms from social workers were directed at lawyers who were not supportive, or who appeared unwilling to listen to and respect the social worker's opinions. Less experienced social workers and those who did not feel they were getting guidance from their own managers were likely to look to lawyers for practical and emotional support and most also wanted them to be strong advocates in court. Lawyers, however, sometimes felt unhappy about being drawn into social work issues, and one described the dilemma they faced: 'It clearly got to the stage where I wasn't advising on legal issues at all … I was trying to prop someone up who wasn't receiving support from their own manager'.

Brammer (2010, page 102) suggests that barriers to effective relationships between social workers and lawyers would be reduced by joint training, multidisciplinary interest groups, dissemination of information such as legal fact sheets, and clarification of roles and responsibilities.

Equally significant as a potential source of tension is the rapid pace of organisational change within social care agencies. Many judges, magistrates and lawyers, and indeed anyone not directly involved in providing social work services, will not be as up-to-date as you are in relation to changes in management structure or terminology and, for example, may continue to regard social services as a generic organisation long after the service was split into separate service areas. You should therefore explain any developments which have affected the responsibilities held by different departments, budgetary decisions, eligibility criteria or how services are planned and delivered.

PRACTITIONER REFLECTION 5.1

In a case in which the mother was looked after by the local authority, the majority of cross-examination of the social worker on behalf of the mother and of the children's guardian was about the services, or lack of them, provided to the mother, even though this was not my team's responsibility. We also get questioned about the services offered by other teams, such as that responsible for adult learning disabilities.

(Child Protection Team Manager)

Relationships with children's guardians

As children's guardians usually come from the same professional background as social workers and are working to the same goal, it might be expected that working relationships between them would be relatively uncomplicated. However, this is not always the case and it is important to anticipate, and thus minimise, potential areas of difficulty, so that they do not detract from the shared aim of achieving the best decision for the child concerned.

PRACTITIONER REFLECTION **5.2**

Courts can appear to have a club-like atmosphere, with much of the business regularly conducted between the same small group of people. As members of that group, children's guardians usually are in good standing with judges and lawyers, whereas social workers tend to be more fleeting visitors who have to prove themselves every time.

(CAFCASS Manager)

RESEARCH SUMMARY

Beckett et al. (2007) found that it was often perceived by social workers that courts gave more weight to guardians' views, even if based on more limited evidence:

'It's almost like the proceedings is the start of involvement. They don't see involvement as being you've tried for years to make a difference with this family. You can give them a load of history ... and it just seems to be wiped away.'

'I've heard the judge say 'This is the expert on the child'. And you just sit there and your blood boils.'

'It's nine times out of ten guaranteed that guardians have more status within the court proceedings than a social worker who has far more contact with the child and the family.'

However, Stanley (2004) found that overt disagreement between professionals was rare, and differences of opinion between children's guardians and local authority social workers tended to be explored and negotiated positively.

Understanding each professional's role, whatever their background, is essential. It is worth, for example, meeting with a children's guardian or local authority lawyer outside any actual legal proceedings, to gain an understanding of their responsibilities and explore potential areas of tension. Also important is an appreciation of the need for far-reaching decisions to be tested by as many means as possible, although this can conflict with the principle of avoiding delay. Ultimately, in many family proceedings there is no *right* answer, or at least little possibility of a result that can be evaluated without the benefit of hindsight, and courts have to accept responsibility for the decisions they make. Beckett et al. (2007) argue that the quality of decision-making, and also, we would add, the challenge of working with others, would benefit from (our italics):

- A less adversarial approach *on the part of everyone, both inside and outside court.*

- Better support for all participants (also highlighted by Dickens, 2006), *particularly service users* (see below).

- Information from the present being seen in the context of what has happened in the past, *particularly by experts, magistrates and judges. Competent social work recording and reporting is essential in this context.*

In addition, Dickens (2006, page 30) concludes, and we agree, that the valuing of difference, rather than its avoidance or suppression, is at the heart of effective inter-professional court work:

> *Differences of opinion and ways of working can be productive, sometimes supporting workers and sometimes challenging them, but always pushing them to reflect on, and account for, their beliefs and practices.*

Most importantly, social workers can enhance their credibility and improve professional relationships by continually working on potential areas of weakness, such as report writing, and being receptive to other points of view.

Reports and files

The next chapters cover case recording and writing reports, and most of your case records will have been written before you find yourself going to court. However, there will always be continuing developments and it is essential that your file is kept up-to-date. It is no good telling the court that you have made recent visits or had contact with other agencies which have not been recorded, or that you have had significant telephone or e-mail exchanges which have not been included in the court papers. Remind yourself of this with this advice: *if it isn't recorded, it didn't happen.*

Support for service users

> *It is very harrowing for people to hear their personal failures discussed publicly. Most clients are very fragile during court hearings and it's difficult to hold them together.*
>
> (Parents' Aid representative)

If you as a professional are anxious about involvement in legal proceedings and attending court, you can imagine how much more daunting it is likely to be for service users. For most of them a great deal is at stake, which may affect their attitudes and behaviour. If, as is likely, there is a disputed issue between you, the traditional social work role as supporter or advocate is unlikely to be possible, and despite your efforts communication may become difficult or non-existent.

> *The first time I went to court it was nerve-wracking. My stomach was turning over ... I thought, oh God, let me get out.*
>
> (Service user, quoted by Booth and Booth, 2004)

Many lawyers are not primarily motivated by a wish to provide emotional support to their clients and they vary in how competent, or interested, they are in this area. Consequently it is not realistic to rely on lawyers or children's guardians to provide high levels of support to service users during court proceedings. Although anything you offer may not be acceptable, it is important to anticipate what might be needed, since lack of support at this point could have far-reaching consequences (see Chapter 11).

> *Children and families may be supported through their involvement in safeguarding processes by advice and advocacy services, and they should always be informed of the services that exist locally and nationally.*

(DfES, 2006, page 190)

RESEARCH SUMMARY

- *Lindley et al. (2001) reported that parents whose children were the subject of child protection plans, and who had received pre-proceedings advocacy support, found that it helped them work with the local authority and facilitated the building of bridges between them. The advocates had a key role in translating jargon, helping explain the nature of the welfare concerns, and providing support at meetings, a particular source of stress.*

- *In several studies reviewed by Hunt (2010), parents reported feeling isolated, unsupported, intimidated, alienated and confused by the formality, language and procedures of court, and were overwhelmed by the number of people involved in their affairs. Where there were a number of hearings, each one tended to reactivate their distress. Many parents had little understanding of how to identify a suitable solicitor and were rarely offered advice in how to go about it. This applied particularly to parents with learning difficulties: 'I went through Yellow Pages, saw the solicitor's name and thought: he sounds like a good one.' (Booth and Booth, 2004).*

- *Brophy et al. (2005) found that among parents of children who were the subject of care proceedings, in addition to the fear that having their parenting called into question would become public knowledge, lengthy statements, use of jargon and long waiting times in public areas added to their stress. Parents often associated family courts with crime, particularly when they shared the same building as criminal courts, and many were unclear about the purpose of different types of hearing.*

- *Research into the operation of rule 9.5 of the Family Proceedings Rules 1991 (Douglas et al., 2006) found that most children were confused by family court proceedings and many parents did not understand the respective roles of the professionals involved.*

- *Research undertaken on behalf of the Children's Commissioner for England (Ofsted, 2010b) found that children disliked having strangers discussing their lives and problems and thought that people would assume they were involved in court because they had done something wrong. They would have welcomed prior information about what was likely to happen, who would be present and how long the hearing would last. Comments made to researchers included:*

  'The court made me feel like an ant against a human.'

  'It seemed as if my life was in the hands of a random group of strangers.'

  'I thought my views and opinions would be taken with a grain of salt and barely heard, much less considered.'

  'I felt I had to say what they wanted to hear.'

Although you may be preoccupied with your own anxieties, a person or organisation skilled in offering help and advice to people who are involved in particular types of legal proceedings can have a significant impact on their experiences and reactions. Frequently, once proceedings have started, service users are left at the back of the court with no one to support them or explain what is going on. In addition, most service users are likely to feel confused and intimidated by the court environment, resulting in high levels of anxiety which make it difficult to ask meaningful questions and retain information.

The research suggests that social workers can do better in terms of anticipating service users' need for support and preparation, even if it is not possible for them to offer it themselves. In addition, social workers may be in a position to mitigate the potentially adversarial atmosphere at court, and to encourage the exercise of more care and sensitivity on the part of others.

A stark warning

Court hearings are never predictable and however well-prepared you are, there is always a risk that something surprising, or even shocking, will occur. In such a situation, you must draw on all your resources to maintain your professional role, and be sure to seek support during supervision afterwards.

PRACTITIONER REFLECTION 5.3

I was sitting behind the lawyers at a hearing in which the local authority was taking care proceedings on the basis of the circumstances surrounding the death of a previous child when, without warning, photographs of the child's post-mortem examination were passed back for everyone to see. I subsequently found it very difficult to concentrate on what was happening in court. I still do not understand why it was necessary for this to happen and of course I now realise that my feelings were nothing as compared with how it must have affected the parents who were in court.

(Social worker)

ONLINE RESOURCES

www.barprobono.org.uk

The Bar *pro bono* unit is a charity which helps find free legal assistance from barristers.

www.clsdirect.org.uk

The Community Legal Service provides advice, a list of legal services providers with the CSL quality mark and a legal aid calculator.

www.citizensadvice.org.uk and its companion website **www.adviceguide.org.uk**

The Citizens' Advice Bureau

www.family-justice-council.org.uk

The Family Justice Council aims to improve the experience of families and children who use the family justice system.

www.lawcentres.org.uk

The Law Centres Federation

www.lawworks.org.uk

Lawworks is the operating name of the solicitors' *pro bono* group. It does not deal with crime, family or immigration matters.

www.legalservices.gov.uk

The Legal Services Commission provides a legal aid eligibility calculator.

www.nyas.net

National Youth Advocacy Service is concerned with children's rights and the provision of socio-legal services to young people up to the age of 25.

Chapter 6
Achieving excellence in case recording

This chapter will help you to meet the following National Occupational Standards for social work.

- Key role 1: Prepare for, and work with individuals, families, carers, groups and communities to assess their needs and circumstances.
  - Review case notes and other relevant literature.
- Key role 5: Manage and be accountable, with supervision and support, for your own social work practice within your organisation.
  - Maintain accurate, complete, accessible and up-to-date records and reports.
  - Provide evidence for judgements and decisions.

Introduction

The case file is the single most important tool available to social workers and their managers when making decisions as to how best to safeguard the welfare of children under their care.

(Laming in DoH and Home Office, 2003, para 6.623)

Bearing in mind how much time social workers spend on recording, it receives scant attention in social work literature and training compared with most other types of skill. Even texts on professional communication, which is essentially what recording is, tend to emphasise verbal, non-verbal and symbolic communication at the expense of writing, although social workers' recording skills have provoked negative comment on occasions.

RESEARCH SUMMARY

Munro's (1996) review of child death inquiries found that more than half criticised the standard of social work records. Lack of baseline details, failure to record who was seen during visits, lack of analysis and cohesion, and factual inaccuracy were particularly noted.

A review of judicial decision-making and the management of care proceedings in Northern Ireland (Iwaniec et al., 2004) found that social work case files often contained a large amount of information about families but lacked a coherent family overview or history. Chronologies were thought by the authors to be necessary, but were often only prepared for court proceedings.

Continued

RESEARCH SUMMARY continued

Inspections of services for safeguarding and looked-after children (Ofsted, 2010) found that unsatisfactory quality assurance systems in some local authorities were compounded by inconsistent and inaccurate recording. In some cases poor recording of decisions leading to foster placements resulted in a lack of effective follow-up support and increased risk of disruption.

Compared with some other professionals, social workers carry a heavy burden in terms of record keeping. After a surgery consultation, a GP may write a prescription or referral letter but in many cases simply takes a few seconds to note the outcome electronically, using accepted abbreviations. School teachers do not note every conversation they have with their students, nor do university lecturers. However, in social work not only do many interviews and meetings last an hour or more, but telephone conversations, e-mail exchanges, discussions with supervisors and managers, meetings and even unsuccessful visits potentially could prove to be significant and must be recorded. However, a disincentive is that recording is almost always less rewarding than actually doing the work, and often there is insufficient time to undertake the analysis and reflection which is necessary to produce clear, relevant, comprehensive and well-structured records.

What is the purpose of social work records?

Social work records:

- Account for work done.

- Provide a framework for ethical practice, including partnership with service users.

- Support assessment, analysis, decision-making, planning, risk management, review and evaluation.

- Ensure continuity.

- Provide a basis for monitoring and evaluating performance.

- Inform strategic planning and research.

- Facilitate effective supervision, reflective practice and continuing professional development.

- Meet statutory and professional body requirements.

- Provide evidence, if required, in formal contexts.

Although this chapter focuses on recording skills which will support you if a case becomes subject to legal proceedings, they are transferable to all of the other categories.

Legal requirements

The law is often used as an excuse not to share information. However, much of it supports information-sharing, providing it takes account of the relevant legal and procedural framework.

ACTIVITY 6.1

Knowledge review

1. *What is the main UK legislation that relates to records, access and data protection?*

2. *List the eight principles of data collection (the circumstances in which you are permitted to keep records).*

3. *Can other professionals remain anonymous when they give you information?*

4. *What should you do if you make an error in recording?*

5. *What does the legislation say about use of jargon or coded language?*

6. *Can a service user insist that you do not record what they have told you?*

7. *How should you respond if a service user asks you to change something in their record?*

8. *Under what circumstances can access to records be refused?*

9. *Is there a right of appeal?*

10. *How long do social work records have to be kept?*

If you do not know any answer, research it and assess whether recording policies and practice in your workplace are clear, consistently applied and take account of legal requirements. In particular, consider how far they anticipate the possibility that records may need to be disclosed in legal proceedings.

Most agencies have policies which support the sharing of records with service users and this principle is supported by legislation. However, in practice they are often ignored. Anticipating the possibility that your records might need to be disclosed to others, and that you may have to defend what you have written, is an effective way of working towards the standards required. Reading other people's recordings with a critical eye and assessing how far they might stand up to challenge will also support the development of your skills.

The Integrated Children's System

This system of recording formed part of the development of children's services following publication by the Department of Health of *Learning the Lessons* (2000). Introduced as a 'conceptual framework, a method of practice and a business process to support practitioners and managers in undertaking key tasks of assessment, planning, intervention and review', it contains templates which form the basis of an electronic social care record.

Pro-formae and templates encourage consistency and uniformity, and electronic recording offers other benefits:

- Information is immediately available, and readable, to people other than the case-holder (for example, out-of-hours service).

- It facilitates the gathering of statistics.

However, there has been debate as to whether the balance between professional and managerial requirements has been correctly struck.

> *The electronic recording and retrieval system does not effectively support staff in undertaking their work. The system is slow and insufficiently robust which leads to time-consuming recording and in some instances work being lost. The combination of no single record for a child and not all files having chronologies makes it difficult to ensure that all historical information is taken into account in assessment and decision-making.*
>
> (Ofsted, 2010a, page 173)

Potential disadvantages include:

- Agenda is not set by the writer.

- Language used may not be what the writer would have chosen, or may be interpreted differently from that which was intended.

- Technical factors may determine the amount or type of information recorded.

- Completing sections which appear to have less relevance to the case in question can be a tedious task.

- Where there are several family members, information may be transferred from one record to another, whether or not it is relevant.

- Important information may be lost if at the time of compiling the record it does not appear to fit any of the sections provided.

- It may be difficult to add to, or change, content.

- Electronic records are often completed in note form, within a loose grammatical framework, which does not provide a good basis for formal reports or witness statements.

- It is difficult to share records with others, particularly service users.

RESEARCH SUMMARY

A review of the Integrated Children's System (Shaw et al., 2009) found that social workers considered templates 'prescriptive, repetitive, bitty and inclined to divide the story into chunks which were difficult to follow'. Specific problems identified were inaccuracy, duplication, reluctance to record information which did not seem relevant at the time, and failure to record dates or return to gaps if information became known subsequently. Some given categories were thought insufficiently precise (for example, 'mental health difficulties'), standard headings lacked flexibility, certain terminology was considered offensive (such as 'parenting capacity') and the forms were often felt to be too complex to be shared with service users.

'You don't get a picture of the child and their needs. It is lost in all these questions and jargon.'

(Social worker)

Continued

RESEARCH SUMMARY *continued*

Overall, it was thought that the system tended to promote 'classified, repetitive and disconnected description' at the expense of 'coherent and specific analysis', and it was suggested that evidence presented within ICS frameworks was not well-received by courts or multidisciplinary arenas.

Notwithstanding these potential constraints, there is considerable scope for managing your records so as to make them fit for their intended purpose, particularly in formal legal settings. Effective written communication involves achieving a synthesis between vocabulary (the words chosen) and how the words are put together (grammar). Professional competence in case recording therefore incorporates both content and style.

Objectivity

One of the central themes of this book is the need to be objective and fair in legal settings, and the way in which you compile your records will strongly influence what you can achieve in this respect. However, since most social work activities are not video- or tape-recorded, it follows that what is recorded is an edited version of events, filtered through the eyes and mind of the writer. A verbatim record of an hour-long interview would run to around 40 typewritten pages, whereas most case recordings are of a page or less, which means that much is omitted and therefore lost, either consciously or unconsciously. In all case recording a degree of bias, arising from ways in which the brain can distort, avoid, select, rationalise or exaggerate experiences in order to support and confirm our beliefs, is inevitable. Anticipating potential sources of bias and taking steps to minimise them will reduce their effect, but they can never be removed altogether. In addition, language is rarely neutral and tends to reflect the values, beliefs, assumptions and prejudices of the writer. Careful choice of words, therefore, can potentially enhance the fairness, and thus professional credibility, of your writing.

Sources of bias in recording include:

Memory

Our brains have insufficient capacity to keep everything in the forefront of our minds and most professionals have to be in command of too much information for it all to be held in their memory simultaneously. We are therefore selective in the information which we attempt to store. Usually the reason we do not recall particular events in detail is because at the time they did not seem important and we made no effort to remember them in order to avoid overload. The busier or more stressed you are, the less remarkable the event appeared at the time, and the longer the period of time that has elapsed since, the less likely it is that you will have detailed recollection without reminding yourself from written records.

When determining accuracy of records in legal contexts, considerable emphasis is placed on the length of time between the event in question and when the record was made. Police officers who did not note an encounter within a few hours of it occurring are likely to have their evidence robustly challenged in a criminal court. Sometimes you need to complete forms with service users and you may also decide to take notes during an interview to act as a prompt later. However, you need to make a professional judgement as to whether this is possible or advisable, taking account of the wishes and feelings of the service user. In addition, taking notes is distracting and may prevent you from observing and listening as carefully as you should. Whether or not you take notes, a delay of even a few hours in making a permanent record makes a significant difference to what is recalled. Your own physical and emotional state will also influence the content and style of what you write.

Perceptual errors

When you form an opinion, you do not take account of what you did not see or hear. The contact supervisor does not hear the whispered exchange that took place behind her back and so, as far as she is concerned, nothing unusual occurred. Yet her perception is false. Perception also involves filtering and stereotyping, so as to make life simpler.

RESEARCH SUMMARY

Munro (2008) found that children's social workers were reluctant to change their perspective on a given case. They tended to interpret new information so that it would fit with their existing analysis; if it was conflicting, it was often disregarded.

'The single most pervasive bias in human reasoning is that people like to hold on to their beliefs.'

(page 137)

We have a psychological inclination to hold on to first impressions (Argyle, 1994), which could lead to inaccuracy and unfairness in recording. Linked to this is a tendency to give more weight to information which fits the view we have formed than to that which does not, and to pay more attention to negative behaviour and events than those which are more encouraging. In the context of recording, this can result in particular facts or events being given unfair prominence, minimised or overlooked altogether.

We all hold preconceptions and it is difficult to read through a file, referral or report from another professional without forming a view of the case concerned. However, like first impressions, once opinions are formed we may be unwilling to modify them and less likely to notice, or appreciate the significance of, subsequent observations and events. A further potential source of perceptual errors is described by Argyle (1994, page 94) as 'attributional behaviour'. He showed that when presented with puzzling events, people tend to make up ('attribute') possible explanations based on their own experience and personality. For example, people who are depressed tend to blame themselves for negative events; if your service user regularly buys large quantities of alcohol, you may be disinclined to believe him when he reports that all his money has been stolen. Your training is intended to ensure that any attributional behaviour on your part is informed by knowledge, skills and values, but in recording your judgements and opinions you should be open to the possibility of subjectivity and, therefore, error in this respect.

ACTIVITY **6.2**

Select a picture, which includes at least two people, from a magazine and devise a story about them (what happened before, what is portrayed, what might happen next) based on your interpretation of their:

- *Gender, age, culture and status.*

- *Physical appearance.*

- *Facial expression.*

- *Clothing.*

- *Relationship.*

- *Surroundings.*

Ask a friend or colleague to do the same and note the similarities and differences in your assessments. What does this tell you about the nature and effects of perception and the influence of stereotyping?

This piece was written by a father who was involved in court proceedings under the Children Act 1989 to determine, among other things, the contact he would have with his child, who did not live with him. The evidence before the court included a social worker's report and the words not in italics are the social worker's interpretation of what the father considered to be the true situation. It is unpublished and was sent to lawyers as part of the father's campaign for more openness and accountability in family courts.

Did the child fall asleep in the car? overtired. *Did the father glance away?* inattentive. *Was there a pause in the conversation?* little to say to each other. *Does the father play with the child?* over-enthusiastic. *Does he not play with the child?* lacking in enthusiasm. *Is the father anxious and apprehensive?* lacks interpersonal skills. *Does he let the child play on the computer?* left to amuse himself. *Does he not let the child play on the computer?* withholds amenities. *Did the father smile?* makes light of the situation. *Has he brought the child a present?* puts pressure on the child. *Did the child laugh and jump on the sofa?* allowed the child to become over-excited. *Did he call the father 'Mr Silly' and try to pull his hair?* no clear boundaries. *Has the father bought toys and other equipment?* trying to set up an alternative home. *Does he miss the child?* emotionally needy. *Does he desperately want to see more of the child?* unable to move forward. *Did the father say he wants to see the child because he loves him?* confuses his own needs with those of the child. *Does he disagree with the social worker?* inflexible. *Does he refuse to produce his medical records?* failing to prioritise the welfare of the child.

This offers a powerful illustration of how a social worker's perception of a series of events was completely at odds with that of the subject of the report.

Figure 6.1 The wings of a butterfly

To reduce the effect of perceptual errors, initially try to treat your opinions as hypotheses that require continued validation to support definitive professional judgements. Good supervision and critical reflection will help you achieve this. It may also help you interpret more accurately if you consider how you would feel if the report in question had been written about you.

Prejudice

Social work's core values do not allow any space for prejudice and it would be good if we could disregard its possible effects. However, we have read plenty of social work reports which confirm its existence (see under Use of language below).

CASE STUDY **6.1**

On returning to her office a social worker was told that a service user had telephoned to apologise for the fact that she had been out shopping when visited earlier, to which the social worker replied, 'Out shoplifting, more likely'.

Only by acknowledging the possibility of prejudice can its effects on attitudes, opinions, and consequently recording, be addressed.

Inexperience, under-developed observation skills or shaky grasp of the subject

Since most social work recording involves noting what has been said and observed, it follows that if you are unsure of what to look for or what is relevant, your records may prove to be unsatisfactory in certain respects, which is likely to be reflected in any evidence you present to court. Similarly, if you are unclear about, or do not accept, the range of theoretical models relative to the case in question, you might find it difficult to decide impartially what to record. For example, a social worker who believed that poverty was the result of the service user's personal inadequacy might fail to take account of, and therefore record, any environmental or institutional factors over which they had no control, but which might be significant. In addition to researching areas of work about which you feel less confident, discussion with more experienced colleagues, together with advice and feedback, will enhance the quality of your records in this respect.

Fact, analysis and opinion

We have heard social workers say that they have been advised to stick to facts when recording, and this is usually the framework for record keeping undertaken by care and support workers. However, in court work social workers are expected to interpret and analyse the facts in order to form a professional opinion. Fact, analysis and opinion therefore all have a place in social work records, although you must distinguish between them so that, for example, opinions are not presented as facts and evidence of analysis is not omitted from professional judgements. Equally important is the need to record reasons for decisions, since they provide the framework for the rationale, which may later be subject to challenge.

When writing your records, it may help you achieve greater clarity if you consider what a lawyer might make of them. If cross-examined in court, how easy would you find it to explain what you meant? The next activity encourages you to think about this.

ACTIVITY 6.3

If you wrote 'X was angry' and it is suggested that they were not angry, how do you convince a court that your assessment is correct? You will find this easier if you support your opinion with evidence of fact: 'When I spoke to X, she replied in a raised voice, with conviction. She said that she was fed up with her son and was not going to continue to pay off his debts'.

What types of fact might be relevant to support the following opinions?

- *When Jake is under stress, he finds it hard to resist pressure from his friends.*
- *There appears to be a lack of parental supervision.*
- *Mrs Qurashi is unwilling to address her alcohol problems.*
- *Amy is reluctant to engage with social care services.*

Clarity of language

The language used in government policy and guidance is often non-specific and imprecise, which does not support good recording skills. For example, the five outcomes contained within *Every Child Matters* (DfES, 2003) convey almost nothing in a legal context, and little in social work terms. If you read that a child was 'enjoying and achieving' or that they were 'making a positive contribution', would you have any idea of what exactly the child was doing? Even more significant in terms of recording, how could progress, or lack of it, be evidenced over time? However, as these examples show, approaching recording through the eyes of others who may wish to challenge its content, whether they be service users or other professionals, can help you to identify where clarification is needed.

ACTIVITY 6.4

From the perspectives of other professionals, particularly lawyers, how would you evaluate the following social worker's report?

'Reason for Initial Child Protection Conference: Ongoing concerns reported from the school regarding:

1. T not wanting to go home;

2. Mum's response;

3. Possible weight loss;

4. T's counsellor feels there is a failure to thrive.'

Comment: The lack of clarity is not only unfair to the subjects of the report, but makes it impossible to form an accurate view of the circumstances of the case. We have rewritten it with the level of detail (hypothetical) which would be sought in any legal arena.

Continued

ACTIVITY **6.4** *continued*

'Reason for Initial Child Protection Conference:

1. On [date] T's head of year (AB) at x school informed CD (social worker) that since September T has sometimes appeared reluctant to go home after school. This is most likely to occur on Fridays.

2. CD visited on [date] to discuss this with T's mother who said she believed T did this to get attention at school and expressed annoyance with her for causing this kind of concern.

3. Since September T's form tutor (EF) has thought that T may be underweight. The school nurse weighed T on [date] when her weight was [y] and her height [z]. The nurse has supplied a report to explain these findings.

4. T has been seeing a counsellor (GH) weekly at school since [date]. GH telephoned CD on [date] to report that since the half-term break [date] T has appeared thin, pale and listless.'

Since records are the primary means by which social workers communicate the facts they have found and the opinions they have formed, it follows that care must be taken to minimise the possibility of ambiguity or confusion on the part of anyone who might read them. Since at the time of writing it cannot be anticipated with any confidence to whom your records will be revealed, records should be fit to be shown to anyone, including service users, managers, inspectors, complaints investigators and other professionals such as lawyers, children's guardians, judges and magistrates.

Use of language

It is not easy to record potentially worrying or negative events without using language which may appear to others as judgemental or even inflammatory. While you must not hesitate to record significant findings, it is often possible to select language which reduces the possibility of your records being regarded as subjective or unfair. However, it can be equally problematic if events are 'repackaged' into euphemisms or jargon which mean little to those outside the profession (see Chapter 7, where we discuss jargon in relation to statements and reports).

Extract from social work record	Comment
Mother was incredibly distressed and hysterical.	'Incredibly' and 'hysterical' are emotive words, with 'hysterical' rarely applied to the male gender. 'The mother was crying and appeared very distressed' might be more objective.
My observations were loud bellowing at the children by the mother's boyfriend.	'Bellow' is a verb usually applied to animals; it is impossible to bellow quietly. A fairer description might be 'the mother's partner appeared angry and shouted at the children'.
Eventually, due to the violence issue, Z escaped to the women's refuge.	'Eventually' does not indicate how long the circumstances had existed. 'Issue' conveys nothing in a legal context and is overused in social work to mask potentially negative behaviour. 'Moved' would convey the message in a less judgemental way than 'escaped'.

Extract from social work record	Comment
Paul looked intimidated.	It is not suggested that Paul said he was intimidated and as such a judgement implies mistreatment by another, it needs to be supported by evidence. 'Apprehensive' is a slightly less prejudicial description; 'frightened' may be more easily understood.
Huge concerns were raised about Aziz, who is the scapegoat of the family.	It is not clear who raised the concerns or what they were. 'Huge' is a conversational word which does not sit comfortably in a professional report. 'Serious' is a possible alternative, but must be related to the precise nature of the concerns. Use of the value-laden word 'scapegoat' is questionable and, without knowing exactly what has happened to Aziz, is insufficiently explicit.
I have attempted to visit Ms Young on numerous occasions without success.	The implication is that Ms Young is being unco-operative, which may be unfair. It needs to be stated how many attempts have been made, when, and whether they were by prior arrangement.

Figure 6.2 *Use of language in social work reports*

Judgement and estimation

Next, there are judgements which it is assumed everyone can make, but which are quite difficult in practice, and may be subjective:

• How tall is the child you have just seen?

• How do you make your estimation?

• Because they are taller or shorter than your own child?

• When you make your assessment, how far away from them are you?

Most people cannot make accurate assessments of speeds, heights, weights and distances and, even if they can, they must remember them in order to record them accurately.

Equally problematic is language used in the assessment of scale. For example, what one social worker may regard as an unacceptably untidy or unclean environment may appear adequate to another, and there is likely to be a range of opinion as to what constitutes a drug or alcohol 'problem'.

ACTIVITY **6.5**

How might you record the exchange below, so as to be fair and objective in quantifying the problem, if there is one? Consider particularly how to convey its tone, the distinction between fact and opinion, and how you might defend your record if necessary. It might be interesting to compare results with a colleague.

SW: I think we need to talk about your use of alcohol, since it seems to be linked to the difficulties you're having with the children. How much would you say you drink on average each week?

Continued

ACTIVITY **6.5** *continued*

SU: Not that much, I've been cutting down. Probably only a few bottles of cider and maybe some lager. It depends on how my day's going. I don't see it's really any of your business.

SW: But you've told me that sometimes you find it hard to get up in the morning and there are quite a lot of bottles over there by the sink. How many would you say you drink on a bad day?

SU: Oh, I don't know, it could be three or four, it could be more. I don't know why you keep going on about it, it's not a crime.

SW: Do you think that's too much?

SU: Not really. Why, do you?

Style

Communicating in writing is not the same as communicating verbally, unless it includes reported direct speech. Most of the case recording we have seen adopts a rather conversational style which is less suitable for formal reports or statements. However, the dilemma is how to balance the need for records to be understood by service users against the possibility that in the future they may assume significance in an inter-professional or legal context. Whether or not it is clear at the time of writing to what purposes the record will later be put, you should exercise the generic writing skills which should achieve clarity and transparency and ensure that your records are fit for scrutiny or challenge.

ACTIVITY **6.6**

Consider how this extract from a social work record could be adapted from its conversational tone:

'Ms D let me in and seemed in quite a state. She shouted at the top of her voice at S who was out at the front playing about on his bike to come in. We chatted in the dining room and the twins were in the lounge watching TV. They came running out, hugging me and grabbing my bag. Then mum put the stair gate on and the twins jumped on the sofa giggling and pushing each other. Mum rushed into the lounge every now and then shouting at them to behave themselves.'

Other stylistic hazards (Hopkins, 1998a) include:

- Repetition: *'the house was in good order and well-maintained'*.
- Overstating the obvious: *'contact will be planned in advance'*.
- Padding: *'expressed the view that'* for *'said'*.
- Empty phrases: *'on an ongoing basis'*.
- Clichés: *'x is on a steep learning curve'*.

- Using passive, rather than active, verbs: *'the opportunity to speak to the grandmother was taken during the visit'.* Changing this to an active verb makes it simpler and saves words: *'during my visit I spoke to the grandmother'.* However, there is a place for passive verbs if you wish to tone down your message or spread responsibility: *'has the baby been fed?'* rather than *'have you fed the baby?'*

Length

The third principle of data protection contained within the Data Protection Act 1998 requires that records should be 'adequate, relevant and not excessive' and, notwithstanding what we have said about the need for clarity and detail, quantity does not usually equate to quality. In most circumstances it is preferable to use the minimum number of words necessary to convey the message. Succinctness will also support you when preparing evidence or being cross-examined, by reducing the amount of material you need to absorb and remember, and making it easier to locate particular sections of the record. Your aim should be to achieve a balance between providing the level of detail necessary to support your professional assessments and the need for records to be focused and concise.

ACTIVITY 6.7

This extract from a social work record has 145 words; we have reduced it by more than half, while retaining all necessary detail.

Sally is a single mum with two children, John aged five and Gemma aged three, she is also currently three months' pregnant. Sally moved into the area with the help of women's aid as the relationship with the children's father was extremely volatile and violent. The three main organisations involved with this case were social care, health and education. However, there were numerous professionals involved, including headmaster of the eldest child's school, allocated social worker for the children, health visitor for the youngest child, midwife for the unborn child, play therapist for the youngest child and parenting counsellors for Sally. The purpose of the team of professionals was to support and develop Sally with her parenting capabilities, help Sally to establish boundaries, and support the children with the emotional conflict and behavioural challenges as a result of witnessing domestic abuse within the family home.

Sally, who is three months' pregnant, is mother to John (5) and Gemma (3). After Sally's relationship with the children's father ended as a result of domestic violence she was assisted with re-housing by women's aid. The professionals currently involved include John's headmaster, Gemma's health visitor, midwife, play therapist, parenting counsellors and social worker. The agreed plan is to support and develop Sally's parenting skills while addressing the children's emotional and behavioural needs.

- Reduce the 60 words below by half and tighten up the expression, while retaining the sense and detail.

The mother, CF, is suffering from a mental health issue and a health issue combined. This has been ongoing and is deemed to be at the root of most of their family issues. Neither her mental health nor medical health issue has been clearly diagnosed, but they are continuing to cause her pain and put strain on her family life.

Grammar

Grammar refers to how words are put together, which influences how easy they are to understand. Once people have left formal education, they tend to assume that they do not need to spend time on developing their ability to write grammatically, and this text cannot assume the role of grammar tutor. However, there are basic rules and it may be helpful to highlight errors which commonly appear in professional social work recording. If you usually record in note form, it can be particularly difficult to adjust your writing to meet the requirements and expectations of formal reports.

- **Weak paragraphing.** Paragraphs are signposts which lead the reader from one key point or topic to the next. Aim to start each one with an introductory sentence, develop the subject and provide a link to the next paragraph. Paragraph length influences the readability of the work.

- **Problematic sentence structure.** Written sentences should be 'units of complete sense' (Lamb, 2010, page 65) containing a subject, object and finite verb. However, varying sentence structure and length by using 'joining words' such as 'and', 'although' and 'also' adds interest and depth to your writing. Common errors are to omit the verb, or use a comma instead of a full-stop prior to starting a new sentence. The best way to detect these kinds of mistakes is to read your work out loud, preferably to someone else. Correct punctuation should ensure that the sense of the sentence is clear.

- **Misuse of apostrophes.** Apostrophes are usually only needed to show that a letter or letters are omitted (as in 'didn't' for 'did not' and 'I'll' for 'I will') or to indicate the possessive case (as in 'Mohammed's son'). Do not add apostrophes to plural words unless they are possessive ('social workers' court skills').

Figure 6.3 Common grammatical errors in social work recording

Letters

In legal proceedings, letters may be offered as evidence that particular information has been conveyed or accepted. As with case recording, templates are often used which carry the same risks inherent in 'cutting and pasting', but also tend to make them appear impersonal and thoughtless (see Michael's story). The language used in letters, even those with a legal purpose, does not have to be stiff and formal, and the emphasis always should be on honesty, sensitivity and simplicity, as shown in the examples below.

Phrase	Replace with
I am in receipt of your correspondence, the contents of which have been noted ...	Thank you for your letter ...
The purpose of this letter is to formally notify you ...	I am writing to let you know ...
In the circumstances we regret that there is no alternative but ...	We have decided ...
Please note that it is the intention of the authority to ...	We are going to ...
If you should wish to discuss the content of this letter, do not hesitate to contact the writer, quoting the above reference.	I am happy to talk to you if anything is unclear.

Figure 6.4 Simplifying the language of letters

You should always sign your letters yourself, unless of course they need to come from someone else for procedural reasons, and provide a reliable means by which the recipient can contact you.

FURTHER READING

Argyle, M (1994) *The psychology of interpersonal behaviour* (5th edition). London: Penguin Books. Contains interesting material on social behaviour and the influence of perception.

Hopkins, G (1998a) *Plain English for social services: a guide to better communication.* Lyme Regis: Russell House Publishing.

Hopkins, G (1998b) *The write stuff: a guide to effective writing in social care and related services.* Lyme Regis: Russell House Publishing.

Both are entertaining books offering guidance, supported by examples, on how to communicate effectively in writing.

ONLINE RESOURCES

www.writeenough.org.uk

Contains an interactive training pack, commissioned by the Department of Health (relevant responsibilities transferred to the Department for Education and Skills) to support good practice in recording. It explains, and provides examples of, key child and family records, including chronologies, genograms, care, adoption and pathway plans.

Chapter 7

Writing formal reports for court

This chapter will help you to meet the following National Occupational Standards for social work.

- Key role 1: Prepare for, and work with individuals, families, carers, groups and communities to assess their needs and circumstances.
  - Review case notes and other relevant literature.
  - Assess needs, risks and options, taking into account legal and other requirements.
- Key role 5: Manage and be accountable, with supervision and support, for your own social work practice within your organisation.
  - Carry out duties using accountable professional judgement and knowledge-based social work practice.
  - Provide evidence for judgements and decisions.

Introduction

This chapter is concerned with reports, which in court may be presented as witness statements.

Reports need to be clear and coherent, using accessible and sensitive language that is non-blaming and evidence-based. They should also produce conclusions that are forward-looking and solution-focused. This doesn't mean avoiding difficult issues but framing them in a way that offers possible solutions.

(CWDC, 2009, p139)

Good, timely assessments and reports from confident and competent social workers, well-supervised, could almost obviate the need to instruct independent social workers, and may reduce the need for other experts.

(Evidence of the Family Justice Council Safeguarding Committee to the Family Justice Review, 25/1/2011, www.family-justice-council.org.uk)

Imagine the judge using your report as a pair of spectacles to bring the evidence into focus.

(Bond et al., 2007, page 79)

The uniqueness of the child should shine out from the page.

(CAFCASS Manager)

Why strive for high standards in reporting to the court?

- To promote the best interests of the child.

- To provide accurate, accessible and relevant information.

- To provide a sound foundation for the action being requested from the court.

- Because well-structured and clearly presented material is the best preparation for giving oral evidence or being cross-examined.

- Because all written material submitted to court is automatically disclosed to all the parties before a hearing.

In the past, social work reports have been criticised for being unfocused, failing to distinguish between fact and opinion, reproducing large sections of case records with little structure or editing and, worst of all, failing to address the best interests of the child (Cooper, 2006, pages 1–2).

RESEARCH SUMMARY

Dickens (2004a) found that a major complaint of local authority lawyers was the amount of time they spent on overseeing the quality of social workers' written statements and reports. They were critical of standards of literacy, but their main concern was the proliferation of unnecessary detail and the inadequacy of analysis. One lawyer said: 'It often just seems a diary of what they have done and that is it. I mean, they have got all that information and you cannot see in the statement how they have come to their conclusion'.

Duty to the court

Unless you are an independent social worker, it is unlikely that you will be asked to act as an expert witness in a formal sense. However, if you are giving evidence in a professional capacity, there is an important technical point. In litigation, witnesses make statements and experts write reports. In family proceedings social workers are experts and so what you write should follow the pattern of an expert's report, even though it may be called a statement.

Although the Civil Procedure Rules do not, for the most part, apply in family proceedings, Part 35 deals specifically with experts and assessors and contains some important provisions. As a matter of good practice, we suggest that you treat these as applying to you as much as to any other expert. The most important is Part 35.3.

(1) It is the duty of experts to help the court on the matters within their expertise.

(2) This duty overrides any obligation to the person from whom experts have received instructions, or by whom they are paid.

This means that when giving evidence as an expert, you are not representing your employer and you are not there to support the case of one party over another. You are there to give your independent view and assist the court towards making a decision, which means that in family cases you have a duty to include everything which might be relevant in deciding what is in the best interests of the child, and to omit nothing. Separate rules apply to experts' reports in criminal proceedings (Part 24 of the Criminal Procedure Rules, 2005).

Write your own statement

This may seem obvious, until you get into the clutches of lawyers. Because of their importance, in the interests of their clients lawyers are keen that reports and statements which are served on other parties before the trial or final hearing should make the best possible impression. This can lead them to want to assist in their production but there is a definite limit to what they may properly do. This limit is widely overstepped, at least in relation to the statements of witnesses of fact, which are often written by solicitors from documents provided to them. Statements should be expressed in a witness's own words and tell the whole story as perceived by them, rather than an edited or massaged version of it. However, if you are not used to giving evidence you may not appreciate what is relevant and what is not. Lawyers can offer guidance on what to include, but they should not determine what you should say.

The Practice Direction to Part 35 of the Civil Procedure Rules, 1999, states that:

2.1 Expert evidence should be the independent product of the expert, uninfluenced by the pressures of litigation.

2.2 Experts should assist the court by providing objective, unbiased opinions on matters within their expertise and should not assume the role of an advocate.

2.3 Experts should consider all material facts, including those which might detract from their opinions.

Paragraph 15.2 of the Protocol to Part 35 is concerned with the influence which lawyers should, or rather should not, have on experts' reports:

Experts should not be asked to, and should not, amend, expand or alter any parts of reports in a manner which distorts their true opinion, but may be invited to amend or expand reports to ensure accuracy, internal consistency, completeness and relevance to the issues, and clarity. Although experts should generally follow the recommendations of solicitors with regard to the form of reports, they should form their own independent views as to the opinions and contents expressed in their reports, and exclude any suggestions which do not accord with their views.

If you are asked if you have written your own statement, you must be able to answer with a confident *yes,* and stand by the statement in its entirety. If other people have made decisions in the case with which you do not agree, you must have the confidence to say so and explain why, otherwise you are likely to face difficulties during cross-examination on your evidence.

Preparation

Reports for use in legal proceedings need to be approached differently from case records or those directed at other professionals. For a busy practitioner, it is tempting to make use of summaries, reviews and other reports when reading up on the history of a case, but prior to writing a report which may have far-reaching consequences, you should read all of the case files and relevant documents. This may involve considerable work, but it is essential to be fully informed before setting out your opinion and the facts as you understand them.

It will help you maintain a balanced view if you have access to good-quality supervision, or at least the opportunity seriously to consider possible alternative viewpoints. This can be difficult once legal proceedings are started, but it is important in terms of establishing a clear rationale for your analysis and opinions.

First steps

As in academic writing, you should prepare a plan, in consultation with your supervisor and legal adviser, to ensure that nothing important is omitted. Similarly, you will need an introduction, followed by the main body of the report, and a balanced conclusion which summarises the main points. You should leave sufficient time to proof-read and edit what you have written before it is disclosed to the other parties, but you also need to ensure that it is completely up-to-date, which may mean adding material at the last minute. If there are any additions, check that they follow logically from, and that there is no repetition or inconsistency with, what you wrote previously; if necessary, cross-refer instead. You will have an opportunity to provide a verbal update at the beginning of any oral evidence.

Ultimately everything which is relied on in court is shown to everyone involved, and although this should happen within formal court processes, it is good practice to try to establish that other parties are prepared for what your report will contain. They may not agree with it, but at least they will have had longer to consider its content, and, if necessary, question you about it, than if it is conveyed via their lawyers close to, or even on, the date of the hearing. However, people who are the subject of reports may not necessarily feel in a position themselves to challenge statements that they regard as inaccurate or unfair.

RESEARCH SUMMARY

A study of parents whose children had been the subject of public law proceedings (Freeman and Hunt, 1998) found that only half received statements and reports in sufficient time to be able to consider them properly.

Concerns about the content of reports emerged in most of the studies of people's experience of public law proceedings reviewed (Hunt, 2010). Criticisms ranged from minor factual inaccuracies, such as names and dates, through words and behaviour being misinterpreted or taken out of context, to allegations of selectivity, exaggeration or even fabrication.

Setting out your report

The front sheet should include the name of the court, case number, names and dates of birth of the people covered by the report, the applicable legislation, your name, professional address and telephone number, and the date and number of the report. It should also be marked as confidential. You should then set out your qualifications and experience in order to establish your credentials; this is a requirement of a formal expert's report. The qualifications should be relevant to your practice as a social worker, starting with the highest, or most recent, first. It is not usual to include qualifications below university level, but if you have completed any relevant specialist training courses, include these together with the dates.

Next, describe your professional experience, including how long you have been a social worker, for whom you have worked and the type of work you have done. If you have relevant specialist experience, or publications or research to your name, these can be included, but you are not supplying an autobiography. At its simplest, you can state how long you have been the social worker responsible for the case and in what connection you are writing your report. If you are formally giving evidence as an expert you must explain why you are writing your report and state whether you have been asked to address a specific issue. CAFCASS advises its staff against including length of experience as it 'risks allowing discrimination against more recently appointed practitioners' (CAFCASS, 2007, page 6). However, this makes assumptions about the existence of judicial prejudice and, as the information is likely to be sought during preliminary questioning in court, the advice could prove counterproductive. Templates for youth justice reports do not allow the writer to give any information about themselves other than name and job title. In this context it is worth considering how you would react to a professional's report which gave no information about the writer.

What to include

In one sense, the title of this section would perhaps be better entitled *What not to include.* A common criticism of social work reports is that every single aspect of the case is included, which can result in important points being obscured by unnecessary detail and make it difficult for the reader to identify the central themes.

If I was to make one criticism of social workers, it is that their written statements and reports tend to be far too long and unmanageable.

(Family court judge)

Too often one is presented with care plans that are as long on rhetorical platitudes as they are short on specific detail.

(Munby, 2004)

The court wants CAFCASS to focus on relevant analysis, not description, to emphasise 'sorting', not 'reporting', and to be brief and specific in style, not discursive.

(CAFCASS, 2007, page 6)

Social workers are not always clear about the issues in the case. For example, they always address placement but often fail to consider contact with extended family. They need to keep the child's future welfare at the forefront of their minds.

(Family court judge)

Obviously it is essential to include all relevant material, but a professional judgement needs to be made as to what this is. A good starting point is to consider your readers: What do they know already? What do they need to know? What is the best way to tell them? It is not likely to be necessary to give a detailed account of everything which has happened since the case first became known to your agency and you should take account of other documents being put to the court, so that information is not duplicated. However, because it is so important, we repeat the fact that you must never omit relevant material which might be prejudicial to your own performance or the result you are hoping for. If you do, you will be vulnerable during cross-examination and may be criticised by the court. Your professional responsibility is to assist the court in relation to the key issues, and a report which addresses them all is more credible than one which is selective (Bond et al., 2007, page 84). A useful test of objectivity is to ask yourself whether you would write the same statement or report if you had been asked to prepare it by one of the other parties to the proceedings.

CASE STUDY 7.1

Re B [1994] 1 FCR 471

In this case the social worker's evidence was criticised as being selective in the material presented and the judge said:

'I cannot emphasise too much that applicants such as a local authority responsible for children in their care ... should not act in a one hundred per cent adversarial way ... they must present [the case] in a balanced way and not fail to refer, it seems deliberately, to factors which point in a direction opposite to that which is desired by the local authority.'

RESEARCH SUMMARY

Research presented at a CAFCASS research conference (Smeeton and Boxall, 2010) sought birth parents' perceptions of social work practice in public law child care and adoption proceedings:

'They tried to win my trust so I would confide in them, so they could use it against me, and that's what they did.'

'They weren't listening to me ... they were like asking for my side of the story, which I was giving them, and they were just writing their own bloody story.'

'From what I can remember there's not one good thing about me [in court statements], it's all about my past and what I'd done wrong and why.'

You should therefore spend time, and include your supervisor and legal adviser, on deciding what needs to be included. Legislation and guidance provide checklists and frameworks to define the scope of assessments and reports, but your aim must always be to focus on, and address, the central issues in the case in a way which is comprehensive, fair, balanced and understandable by all involved. A preset agenda for the structure and content of reports is not usually as helpful to the court as it may be to you, and it may discourage you from providing the depth of professional analysis which the court ultimately seeks.

PRACTITIONER REFLECTION 7.2

Social workers tend to follow a formula, and I can see that structure matters. In other words, nothing is left out. On the other hand, sometimes there is very little individual comment in the report. It is mostly the standard questions and answers and it often looks far more substantial than it is.

(Family court judge)

As we have seen in the previous chapter, a further potential pitfall arising from using checklists and templates is that you may be tempted to 'cut and paste' some of the content, which, apart from compromising the individuality and objectivity of the report, carries the risk of potentially serious consequences.

Well, half of it relates to my children but then there are names and details of children in the report that I don't recognise.

(Parent, quoted by Broadhurst and Holt, 2010)

After listing the sources you have used, it is usually sensible to start by explaining who everyone is. Diagrams such as ecomaps and genograms can be used to explain complex family situations but this kind of tool takes time to prepare and must be presented to a high standard to be effective. You also need to list anyone outside the family who is referred to in the report, such as a teacher, health visitor or support worker.

Avoid writing a suspense novel

It is usually helpful to those who will read your report if you provide a synopsis of your final conclusion at the outset (Bond et al., 2007, page 88). This enables the reader to place in context the facts and opinions included, as they progress through the report. It may also help you to avoid incorporating extraneous or irrelevant material.

Chronologies

A chronology provides the court with a list of key events and is required in public law applications. Chronologies should be sequential, concise, contain no analysis, opinion or professional judgement, and identify essential facts which are accepted by all parties. They also need to be up-to-date.

CASE STUDY 7.2

A social worker's first experience of compiling a chronology:

Initially I thought the task would be quite simple but I was surprised by how much information I had to skim read. The case had lots of significant negative events which I had to include. However, I was clear that a chronology should represent facts, not opinion, which included events that demonstrated the parents' strengths. I needed to avoid judgements and keep my values separate from the facts. The exercise showed me how important it is to keep files well-ordered and up-to-date, and also that a chronology can support assessment and analysis, in that patterns of behaviour or events may emerge.

Fact, analysis and opinion

As social workers are regarded by the courts as experts, they are expected to analyse the facts to form professional opinions, just as other professional witnesses do. Indeed, any reluctance to do so may be regarded as lack of competence or credibility as a witness. However, a note of caution: when you express an opinion, you must only do so within the limits of your own expertise. This is particularly important if evidence from other professionals would normally be sought before a conclusion is reached, as in a case of possible sexual abuse or in relation to the physical development of a child. If you have only worked on a very few cases in which sexual abuse was suspected, then your opinion needs to be far more tentative than if you have had many years' experience of such cases. Similarly, interpretation of material such as growth and weight charts must be presented by a suitable health professional. You should also avoid using expressions taken from other disciplines, such as medical or psychiatric diagnoses, unless it can be shown that they were originally made by a person properly qualified to do so.

CASE STUDY **7.3**

> *Direct work with a child to ascertain her 'wishes and feelings' was undertaken primarily by a family support worker who knew the child well and with whom she had established a good rapport. However, she was not trained to interpret, analyse or form professional judgements from what she had observed; consequently the court was left with a great deal of descriptive material from which they could deduce very little.*

Professional opinions expressed in a report should always be based on analysis of material contained in that report. Everyone who reads it should be clear on what facts your opinion is based, to what extent you have personal knowledge of those facts and the source of any facts of which you do not have personal knowledge, such as case records made before you took over the case. If you are not the first person to have worked on a case, it may be helpful to follow the summary of how the case was presented when you took it over with what you thought about it after you had got to know something about it, and why you formed the view that you did. It is also sensible to record that you have reread your own case records to remind yourself of the details of your involvement. When referring to facts within your own knowledge, it is usually best to tell the story chronologically. There may be themes that you wish to cover separately, such as the involvement of a particular family member, substance misuse or the local authority's plans, but it is easiest to follow a story if it is told in the order in which events happened.

In general you should avoid being dogmatic in expressing an opinion, unless you strongly believe that there is only one possible view. However, if there is no dispute about what has happened or should happen, it is unlikely that there would be a court hearing. It is much more likely that there is a range of options for the court to consider and it is good practice to, and if you are instructed as an independent expert you must, describe the range of opinion on the issue in question.

Although the court needs to know what your opinion is, it is, if anything, more interested in how you came to form your opinion. In other words, what facts did you take account of, how did you interpret and analyse them, and what other options did you consider? The formulation of this rationale should, we suggest, incorporate four further Rs:

- **Reading** – about any relevant theories; for example, attachment and loss.

- **Research** – into 'what works' in cases with factors similar to the one being tried; for example, how to ensure that a permanent placement of a child of a particular age has the best prospect of success. However, if you refer to research, you must present a properly referenced and balanced overview (see below).

- **Resources** – what resources are required and are available to support the plan proposed; for example, the realistic prospects of a specialist residential placement being available, and funded, within a reasonable period of time.

- **Reflection** – testing, stretching and analysing your thinking, so as to promote self-awareness, objectivity and confidence in professional decision-making.

Figure 7.1 *Rationale*

If you have not got a rationale for your opinion, you should not be expressing it. Sometimes, in highly technical cases, judges manage to get away with rather woolly reasons for their opinions; for example, a judge who must choose between contrasting expert evidence may go for one opinion rather than another because the outcome seems fairer, without being able to explain in sufficient detail to satisfy the respective experts what was unsatisfactory about the rejected evidence. Unfortunately, that soft option is not available to you. Courts are keenly interested in the reasons for your opinion, and that of any other expert, and want to understand them so they can decide rationally on the best course to take.

You must make it clear if you do not feel you have all the relevant facts with which to form an opinion, and also if your opinion is based on disputed facts of which you have no personal knowledge, and your opinion would be different if an alternative version of the facts was found to be correct. If you wish to qualify your opinion, you must explain why. You also need to be able to explain and justify the process of analysis which led to the formation of your opinion. Usually it will be based on your own knowledge and experience, which you will be able to describe, but if you wish to refer to research it is wise to discuss it with your legal adviser, since there are potential pitfalls and it is likely to be a time-consuming exercise. Nevertheless, as in academic writing, you must reference any definitive statement which falls outside your personal knowledge or experience. If you intend to rely wholly, or partly, on published research, you should clearly state this and attach the relevant article(s) to your report. You must also seek out any relevant published material which may not support your view, attach copies, and explain why your opinion is different. Again, if you do not, you risk being exposed in cross-examination or criticised by the court. You should also consider whether any documents should be attached to your report, such as plans, letters or agreements made with the family. However, if these are of questionable quality or validity, they may have the opposite effect to that intended.

ACTIVITY **7.1**

In the context of what we have said about using research, what is unsatisfactory about these extracts from reports?

- *'If the move to a permanent placement is handled with sensitivity and good planning, such a placement will not have long-lasting detrimental effects on J's further development.'*

- *'Research has shown that children who witness domestic violence are often described as the "forgotten victims" (***www.hiddenhurt.co.uk***).'*

- *'Men who are violent to their female partners are also likely to be violent to their children. The overlap between men's violence towards women and the physical abuse of children is estimated as in the range of 30–60 per cent (Eldeson, 1999).'*

The first example makes a vague but definitive statement without providing any evidence to support it. The social worker needs to explain what 'sensitivity' and 'good planning' actually mean in the context of the case and possibly refer to research into the effects of a further move on children with the age, family circumstances and history of the child in question. The second example is insufficiently specific about the research referred to, which in any case does not appear to be of any use to a court deciding a child's future. The name of the website suggests that it is unsound academically; in fact it was found to be the work of a victim of domestic violence which carries the warning that 'the information is neither comprehensive nor infallible'. Consequently it is of no assistance to a court and undermines the professional credibility of the writer. The third extract quotes statistics which are out of date and of too wide a range to be useful. As the writer did not provide a bibliography, the information cannot be verified. Remember, too, that anything you write in this context should be understandable to service users, which may include children and young people.

Use of language

One of the most important aspects of presenting evidence, whether written or oral, is use of language. In court work, as in other professional contexts, language should be a means, and not a barrier, to communication and a report which uses language which is vague, confusing, lacks rigour or contains jargon, acronyms or clichés is likely to land you in considerable difficulty, particularly when being cross-examined. Judges also cherish brevity and clarity (Bond and Sandhu, 2005). For some reason social workers do not have a particularly good reputation when it comes to use of language. They seem inclined to take ordinary words and phrases and surround them with a mystique which leads to barriers to understanding and can be a gift to a cross-examining lawyer. This is illustrated by the following story, which was told to us by a student social worker who observed the event on placement.

CASE STUDY **7.4**

While visiting a man to assess his need for community care services, the social worker explained that the aim of the resulting care plan was to empower him, to which he replied: 'That's very kind of you, but I don't need to be empowered as I've just signed up with British Gas'.

Other examples are the service user who thought that the word 'case conference' meant that everyone attending the meeting would be carrying a briefcase, and another who understood 'eligibility criteria' to be something to do with joining a dating agency. Even words in common use, such as 'partnership', can be understood differently in different contexts. We once observed a social worker struggling to explain to a judge what the description 'keyworker' meant. When she finished, the judge observed drily, 'I see; so it has nothing to do with keys then?' Not, perhaps, a major error, but it does not inspire confidence in social workers' ability to express themselves clearly and concisely. It can also make service users feel excluded and confused at a time when they are facing many unfamiliar and often frightening experiences.

PRACTITIONER REFLECTION **7.3**

I would like social workers to tell me in plain English what they really think. Far better to say that they found the mother 'fed-up and difficult', and describe the facts which led to this conclusion, than some bromide expression like 'Mrs Smith's co-operation was a little lacking'.

'Behaviour issues' could mean anything from a tendency to fidget to a propensity to arson.

'Kevin has difficulty relating adequately to his peer group' just means he hasn't got any friends.

(Family court judges)

Lawyers can sometimes appear to non-lawyers to be overly concerned with use of language. However, a substantial part of their work involves determining the meaning of specific words or phrases. Unclear language in a will, lease or contract of employment, for example, can lead to disputes which require a considerable amount of unravelling (as in the proverbial will containing only the words 'All To Mother'). It follows, then, that any ambiguity or lack of clarity in reports or evidence is likely to attract the court's attention. In fact, there is really no excuse for using language which is likely to lead to misunderstanding, confusion or exclusion, either in or out of court. It would do so much for both social worker/lawyer and social worker/client relations if social workers were to express themselves clearly, concisely and, above all, simply.

'Avoid jargon like the plague.' (Family court judge)

The next examples are designed to help you think about the language you use and devise ways to improve your expression. It is impossible to overemphasise the importance of this in the court setting. The first concerns the use of jargon. Jargon is a form of shorthand in which pseudo-technical vocabulary is used to make things sound more important (as in 'sibling', instead of 'brother' or 'sister'). It is also a way of repackaging ordinary events to fit within particular professional categories, theories or values. What it actually does is create barriers, emphasise power differentials and make it difficult or impossible for those who are not in on the secret to understand what is meant. Once you have got into the habit of using jargon, it is very difficult to stop. It is something of a mystery to us why social workers are so prone to using jargon. It might have something to do with lack of professional confidence, or it may be picked up from the style of language now used in many official communications. Sometimes it represents an attempt to obscure the reality of a situation, or to remove potentially negative connotations, as in 'behaviour issues'. Whatever the reason for its use, it does not accord with basic social work values. If what you say or write cannot easily be understood by other professionals or, even more importantly, service users whose interests should be central to your practice, then you are not meeting basic professional standards. Having said this, we acknowledge that lawyers certainly are not blameless in this respect. Some of the most commonly used legal terms are described in Chapter 3 and if you encounter legal expressions or acronyms that you do not understand, you should not hesitate to ask for clarification. You might also reflect on how it feels to be excluded in this way.

ACTIVITY 7.2

The following expressions, all of which come within the definition of jargon, have been included in social work reports. Reword them so that they are easier to understand.

- *Care package*
- *Team around the child*
- *Positive outcome*
- *Respite care (we have seen this written as rest-bite, which shows that social workers are sometimes confused by their own jargon)*
- *Care programme approach*
- *Core assessment*
- *Creative solutions panel*
- *Age-appropriate self-care skills*

Acronyms are widely used in professional contexts, but they have the same exclusive effect as the use of jargon.

CASE STUDY 7.5

A student on placement in a children's team attended a meeting during which there were repeated references to what he thought were 'lack forms'. He decided that these must relate to recording shortcomings in respect of the care a child was receiving, but later discovered that what were being referred to were LAC (Looked After Children) forms.

When you are compiling reports for use in legal proceedings, or preparing a statement of evidence, ensure that you do not use acronyms without first explaining them fully. It would be better still if you did not use them at all.

Clarity of language

Equally likely to get you into difficulty in legal contexts is the use of imprecise language.

CASE STUDY 7.6

'The children were inappropriately dressed'.

This short sentence gives rise to more than a dozen potential questions about its meaning and would be a gift to a cross-examining lawyer.

- *What clothing are you referring to (underclothes, nappies, nightclothes, outdoor clothes, shoes, school clothes)?*

Continued

CASE STUDY **7.6** *continued*

- *In what way was it inappropriate?*

  For their age (no clean nappies for a baby)?

  For the weather (T-shirt in the middle of winter)?

  For the time of day (pyjamas in the afternoon)?

  Standard of cleanliness (smell of urine)?

  Worn out (torn coat)?

  Ill-fitting (shoes too small)?

  Lack of supervision (slippers in the garden)?

  A health or safety risk (barefoot, with broken glass on the floor)?

- *How many children are included in the description?*

- *What age are they? (in terms of welfare, clothing is more significant for a baby than a teenager)*

- *Does the description apply equally to all the children?*

- *For how long, and how often, have you or others made this observation?*

- *Have you discussed it with the parent/carer?*

- *What was their response?*

As in case recording, imprecise references to time, such as 'during the summer holidays' or 'at the weekend', should also be avoided.

Respect

An essential element of respect is taking care to spell people's names correctly and avoiding factual errors in relation to matters such as dates, addresses, moves, relationships, schools, employment and medical details. If these are found to be incorrect they can potentially undermine your professional credibility in the eyes of the court, and to service users mis-spelt names represent lack of professional care at its most basic (Hunt, 2010, page 22).

When you refer to adults in your report or statement, use their name and title ('Miss Tanya Smith'), rather than their role ('Mum'), which is patronising and denies their existence in any respect other than the position in question. It is also usually helpful to explain, at least at the first mention, the relationship of anyone outside the immediate family ('Mr Singh, the children's paternal grandfather').

While you should not hesitate to present the facts as you know them, sensitive use of language when dealing with contentious matters can make a difference to the experience of service users and possibly the prospects of being able to establish workable professional relationships with them in the future. This is particularly important in the context of what one party may have said about or done to another, or when dealing with an issue on which there are strongly opposing views. Care taken in this context will also encourage the court to regard all your evidence as fair and balanced.

Presentation

Anyone involved in court proceedings has to assimilate a large amount of written material. As first impressions are influential, it follows that anything which is poorly presented will attract attention and may result in a negative judgement of its writer which is hard to reverse. Hopefully, it goes without saying that reports should be free of grammatical and spelling errors. If you know you are at risk of making these, you must allow sufficient time to have your report checked by someone else. Numbered pages and paragraphs, each of which should refer to one main point, make it easier to refer to specific sections, and many courts request wide margins and double line spacing so that notes can be added. In academic writing, students are sometimes advised that subheadings impede the flow, but in a long report they can be useful signposts, particularly if they are numbered and indexed at the beginning. Any additional material included should be separately listed so that the whole document is easy to navigate.

Statement of truth

Witness statements made in proceedings to which the Civil Procedure Rules apply must contain what is called a statement of truth: 'I believe the facts stated in this witness statement are true'. This may seem simply a formality, but making a false statement verified by a statement of truth, without an honest belief in the truth of the statement, is contempt of court. You should therefore take great care that everything in your statement is accurate before signing a statement of truth.

Additional requirements for formal experts' reports

A formal expert's report is addressed to the court, not the party which has commissioned it. In addition to the matters already considered, it must contain a summary of conclusions, a formal statement that you understand your duty to the court and that you have complied with it, and a statement of truth, the wording of which is slightly different from that attached to an ordinary witness statement: 'I confirm that I have made clear which facts and matters referred to in this report are within my own knowledge and which are not. Those that are within my knowledge I confirm to be true. The opinions I have expressed represent my true and complete professional opinions on the matters to which they refer'.

Probation and youth justice reports

Reports by probation and youth offending teams in respect of people convicted in criminal courts are, of course, expert's reports, but must comply with Home Office National Standards for the Management of Offenders, 2007, or the National Standards for Youth Justice Services, 2010.

Youth Justice Standard 5 offers general guidance on written and verbal court reports which should be:

- Balanced and impartial.

- Timely.

- Focused and analytical.

- Free from discriminatory language and stereotype.

- Verified and factually accurate.

- Understandable to the child or young person and their parents or carers, who should have the opportunity to read and ask questions about the report before it is presented in court.

- Sufficiently informative and analytical to enable courts to make informed decisions regarding sentencing.

Specific additional requirements are:

- A list of sources of information.

- Offence analysis, including the impact of the offence on the victim.

- Assessment of the young person leading to a proposed intervention.

- Assessment of the need for parenting support.

- Assessment of the risk to the community, including the likelihood of reoffending and risk of harm to others.

- Conclusion and proposal for sentencing.

Probation National Standards allow little scope for initiative, as the content and layout of each type of report is clearly prescribed. As we have seen, one of the disadvantages of this, as with assessment frameworks and other types of checklist, is that you may concentrate on covering all the required factual issues at the expense of presenting a clearly argued professional opinion.

Probation National Standards appear to contemplate slightly different approaches to different types of report: a bail information report should be 'objective, factual and impartial', while a pre-sentence report is to be 'objective, impartial, free from discriminatory language and stereotype, balanced, verified and factually accurate', and a specific sentence report is not required to have any of these qualities. However, we think it is clear that probation and youth justice reports should comply with the standards of witness statements and reports discussed in this chapter.

A final word

If you are writing a statement or report, all you can really do is tell the story as you perceive it, as fully as you can. However, if you are offering professional analysis and opinion, you want the court to take notice of it. We have read many witness statements and experts' reports, which can run to tens, or even hundreds, of pages and require a high level of concentration and dedication on the part of the reader. You are more likely to make an impact if what you have written is well set out, clearly signposted, structured, focused and interesting. You don't want the readers wondering whether you are ever going to get to the point.

Cooper, P (2006) *Reporting to the court under the Children Act* (2nd edition). London: Stationery Office.

Contains advice, examples and checklists to help those preparing local authority statements and reports.

NACRO (2003) *Pre-sentence reports for young people: a good practice guide* (2nd edition). London: NACRO.

www.ewi.org.uk

The Expert Witness Institute provides a template for expert witness reports.

www.scie.org.uk/elearning/index.asp

Contains an interactive courtroom case study, based on social work reports.

www.yjb.gov.uk

Standard 5 of National Standards for Youth Justice Services relates to reports for courts and youth offender panels.

Part 3
Attending court

Chapter 8
Court rules, etiquette and practical matters

This chapter will help you to meet the following National Occupational Standards for social work.

- Key role 5: Manage and be accountable, with supervision and support, for your own social work practice within your organisation.
  - Carry out duties using accountable professional judgement and knowledge-based social work practice.

- Key role 6: Demonstrate professional competence in social work practice.
  - Review and update your own knowledge of legal, policy and procedural frameworks.

Introduction

Here we support advice on preparation by explaining court layout and practical matters, including how to address judges, what lawyers wear, the order in which things happen, confidentiality and relations with other parties. We also introduce further legal rules which affect the conduct of court proceedings. Rules can be daunting if you do not understand them but they also offer structure, consistency and a degree of predictability.

ACTIVITY **8.1**

Ask colleagues or friends what they know about court rules.

- *What is the source of their information?*
- *What connotations does it have for them?*
- *What do they consider is their purpose?*
- *What do they think will happen if any of the rules are not followed?*   *Continued*

- *If they were a witness, what would concern them most in relation to court rules?*
- *Where would they go for help in understanding them?*

Compile a list of the most common responses. This will provide you with a framework with which to prepare and support others involved in court proceedings.

What does a court look like?

Hearings in open court

You probably have an idea of what a courtroom looks like from films or television. At the front is a long desk (*bench*) where the judge sits facing everyone else. In Victorian courts it may be as much as six feet above the rest of the room, but in modern courts it is usually only slightly higher. The judge's entrance is behind or beside the bench, in front of which are tables for the clerk, usher and lawyers. In modern courts the front row is for QCs, if there are any, the next is for junior barristers and behind them sit solicitors. QCs do not

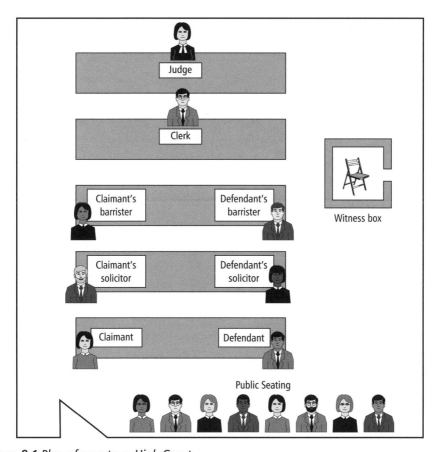

Figure 8.1 *Plan of county or High Court*

usually appear in county or magistrates' courts, so these courts usually have two rows of tables. In criminal courts the dock is likely to be opposite the witness box, with a separate entrance from the cells below. In crown courts the jury sits in two rows of seats at the side of the court. There are usually seats reserved for the Press and, in criminal courts, probation and police liaison officers. In civil courts the claimant's lawyers normally sit to the left with the defendant's lawyers on the right, as you face the judge. In crown courts the prosecution lawyer is furthest away from the jury, with the defendant's lawyer nearest to the jury.

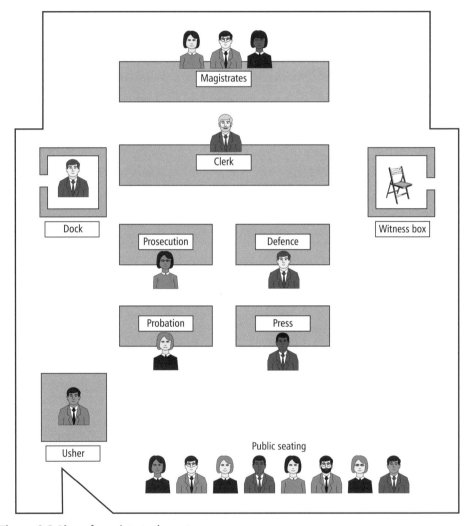

Figure 8.2 *Plan of magistrates' court*

Private hearings in the county or High Court

Private county court hearings are usually held in a room like an office. The judge sits at a desk, with a table in front for the lawyers and anyone else involved in the case. Some county court hearings and private hearings in the High Court take place in an ordinary courtroom from which the Press and public are excluded.

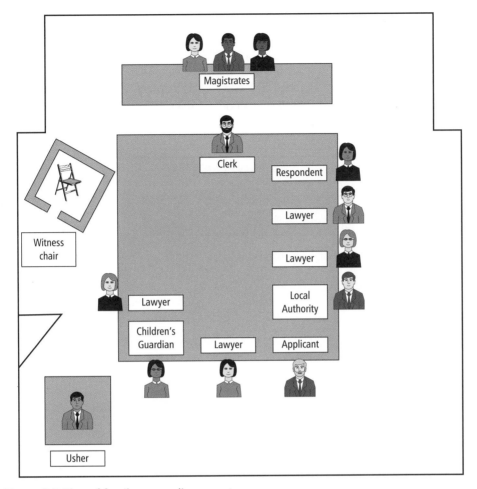

Figure 8.3 *Plan of family proceedings court*

Family courts

The layout of a magistrates' court sitting as a family court is similar to that of a county court district judge's room.

Youth courts

Magistrates' youth courts are arranged differently from other criminal courts, to make them less intimidating for young people (see Figure 8.4).

What do judges wear?

Judges never wear in court the elaborate ceremonial robes seen on formal occasions, so you will not see them in long wigs, breeches and stockings except on television. Until recently court business was either conducted in open court or *in chambers*, which could be in the judge's room or a courtroom. Most of the business conducted in chambers was not actually private, although the size of the room meant that not many people could attend. For hearings not in open court, judges and lawyers wear ordinary suits. For formal hearings in open court, such as trials, judges and lawyers usually wear robes. In 2008 a civil robe, designed by Betty Jackson, was introduced for some judges conducting civil trials: circuit judges were not included as a cost-saving measure. It is black, closed at the front and worn without a wig or collar, with different levels of judge being identified by means of different coloured tabs at the neck.

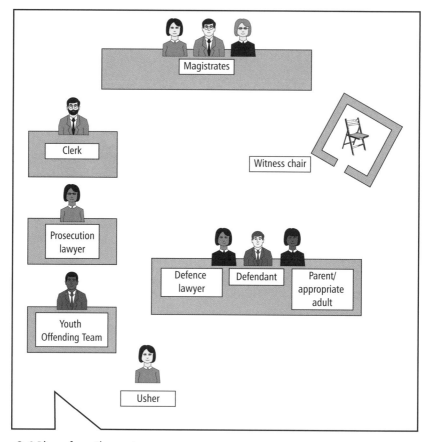

Figure 8.4 *Plan of youth court*

District judges in open court wear the civil robe with blue tabs. For other hearings they wear ordinary suits, as do Masters. In open court Masters wear the civil robe with pink tabs.

Recorders and Deputy High Court judges who are barristers wear the robes they normally wear in court.

Circuit judges in criminal trials wear violet robes, rather like dressing gowns, over ordinary clothes, a short judges' wig and, if male, bands and a wing collar. Over the left shoulder is a red sash. In civil trials circuit judges dress as in criminal trials but with a lilac sash and without wig or bands.

High Court judges conducting civil trials wear the civil robe with red tabs.

Queen's Bench Division judges wear red robes in criminal cases, with fur facings in the winter and silk facings in the summer.

Court of Appeal judges in criminal cases wear a court coat and waistcoat with skirt or trousers and bands, a black silk gown and a short wig. In civil cases they wear the civil robe with gold tabs.

Supreme Court judges only ever wear lounge suits.

What do lawyers wear?

Junior barristers' court dress is a black gathered gown, wig and, if male, a wing collar and bands, worn over an ordinary suit.

QCs wear a black tail coat and waistcoat over trousers or a skirt, or a sleeved waistcoat which has no tails and is more practical. They wear the same wig, collar and bands as junior barristers but their gown is not gathered and originally was made of silk, which is why being appointed a QC is sometimes referred to as *taking silk*. Most QCs now wear a rayon gown which is cheaper and more hard-wearing.

Solicitors' when robed, wear bands and a wing collar, if male, and a black gown which is different from either of the barristers' gowns.

ACTIVITY 8.2

A barrister's view on wearing wigs (letter to *The Daily Telegraph*, 15 January 2007):

'Wigs disguise judges and have the additional benefit of obscuring how decrepit they are. I sat as a deputy judge to enforce a maintenance order, substantially in arrears. For this purpose, I had to wear my wig. The delinquent husband was not pleased with my order and for months afterwards mounted a one-man picket outside the Royal Courts of Justice bearing a placard that stated his opinion of me in no uncertain terms. Often when doing my day job as a barrister, I had to pass right in front of him in order to get into the building. He did not recognise me once.'

'I wanted wigs off because they are really scary' (Young witness quoted by Plotnikoff and Woolfson, 2009, page 93)

What advantages and disadvantages do you see in lawyers and judges wearing robes from the point of view of the users of courts (litigants, witnesses, people facing criminal charges, jurors, experts, other professionals)? Consider your reaction to other situations in which people wear uniforms: hospitals, police stations, care homes, schools, airports, churches.

How do you address a judge?

Bearing in mind how many different types of judge there are, this is reassuringly simple. At all levels below recorder, and in magistrates' courts and tribunals, use *Sir* or *Madam*. Recorders and circuit judges are addressed as *Your Honour* and judges in the High Court, Appeal Court and Supreme Court are *My Lord* or *My Lady*.

What do you do when you get to court?

This depends on why you are there, and in particular on whether you have to be available to discuss the case with lawyers or to give evidence. In most cases social workers have to do both. You may also attend criminal courts to provide reports or support service users.

Pre-trial conference or consultation

On the first day of a hearing there is usually a conference or consultation before the hearing starts. The lawyers may have some last-minute thoughts to discuss with you, or there may have been developments which they need to know about. We advise that you arrive at court at least half an hour before the hearing is due to start, although earlier may be suggested.

Negotiations

In ordinary civil litigation the emphasis is on settling the case if at all possible, but it is often only on the day of the hearing that any of the parties turn their minds sensibly to the possibilities of settlement, which may have something to do with recognising the risks of failure. In family cases involving children, settlement is not achievable by the parties alone as the approval of the court is needed, which may mean that it is not until the hearing approaches that anyone, including the lawyers, gives serious thought to the possibilities of compromise. You should therefore allow time for negotiations before the hearing begins. If you are the case social worker your participation in these, at least at the level of being able to discuss proposals with the lawyers, is essential. You may also find that the court agrees to delay the hearing so that further discussions can take place. However, these kinds of negotiations can pose difficulties for social workers.

PRACTITIONER REFLECTION **8.1**

Lawyers, and to some extent guardians, seem happy to conduct the majority of their business at court. Social workers and their managers are often placed under pressure to negotiate or make decisions which either they do not have authority to make, or which require resources which they are not able to guarantee are available.

(Child protection team manager)

It is important that the lawyers understand the decision-making process in your agency and you should try to ensure that a responsible manager is with you in court, at least for the start and expected end of the hearing.

Confidentiality

A common practical problem is how to maintain confidentiality. Courts do not usually have much interview space and it is common for discussions to take place in public areas. Knowing that their affairs would be discussed by strangers and having to wait around in a public place are major concerns of both adults and children whose circumstances have been the subject of court proceedings (Brophy et al., 2005; Ofsted, 2010b). If possible, you should insist that people's private business is not discussed in places where it can be overheard. If, as is likely, it is anticipated that there is no room available at the court, other arrangements need to be planned for negotiations or discussions. However, even if rooms are available within the court building, you still need to be alert to the potential for breaches of confidentiality.

> *I was taken through another waiting room, which was empty at the time. When I left the interview room, there was a couple outside. I apologised for interrupting them and they replied: 'Don't worry, it was very interesting listening to your conversation'.*

> (User of family court, quoted in HMICA, 2008)

> *The waiting room was small with other witnesses there for other cases. There was nowhere private to go, only the toilet, one between all of us.*

> (Parent of young witness quoted by Plotnikoff and Woolfson, 2009, page 78)

Attending the hearing

Lawyers want someone who can react responsibly to what is happening to be in court throughout the hearing. In particular they need someone who can comment on what is being said on behalf of another party. If you are the case social worker you are best equipped to do this, and so you should expect to attend the whole of every day of the hearing. If you are instructed as an independent expert you will probably have to attend court during any factual evidence relevant to opinions you have expressed. If anything emerges which causes you to change or modify your opinion you must tell the lawyers who instructed you. You should also do this if you are the case social worker and wish to alter anything contained in your witness statement. You will almost certainly, either as an independent expert or the case social worker, be asked to comment on any expert evidence called on behalf of other parties and to suggest possible lines of questioning. If you are an independent expert, it does not compromise your independence to inform your client's lawyer of any fallacies you see in another expert's opinion. However, you are not an advocate for your client, and professional embarrassment of another expert is not a proper aim, however tempting it may be.

The atmosphere in court

All court proceedings are fairly formal, although magistrates' courts tend to be less so than higher courts. However, the degree of formality can be daunting if you are not familiar with it, and for service users it can present a formidable barrier (Hunt, 2010).

ACTIVITY *8.3*

In relation to a decision-making forum with which you have been involved, assess how far the degree of formality influenced the following essential aspects:

- *Adhering to a clear agenda.*
- *Ensuring that everyone has a chance to contribute effectively.*
- *Keeping the discussion focused on the task.*
- *Providing the opportunity for negotiation.*
- *Dealing with conflict.*
- *Keeping within a reasonable timescale.*
- *Reaching a decision.*
- *Deciding the means by which the decision will be implemented and evaluated.*

What does this tell you about the value, or otherwise, of formality in court proceedings?

Whether to bow

At the start of a hearing or on entering court, everyone used to be expected to bow towards the judge or magistrates as a mark of respect. You will see that lawyers and court staff still do this, although often it is little more than a brief nod of the head. Increasingly in civil courts, parties and witnesses are not expected to bow, although it is still common in criminal courts.

Humour

Occasionally court proceedings have their lighter moments. Some cases which revolve around rather dry questions of commercial law can be quite boring, even for the paid participants. There is a game which barristers used to play, in which the challenge was to use a word chosen by colleagues without the judge recognising the alien concept. One of us successfully introduced the word *hippopotamus* into a case about wheat farming in Norfolk and if the judge noticed he was not brave enough to say. Most humour is unintended, however. When judges were less familiar with popular culture, they sometimes caused amusement by asking questions like *Who are The Beatles?* or, in a case in which one of us was involved, *What is a twin-tub washing machine?* However, most judges today are reasonably in touch with ordinary life and fortunately such embarrassing remarks are rare.

In some proceedings, especially those involving children, the judge and lawyers usually try to relax the atmosphere in order to make the experience less intimidating. However, you should take your lead from them. In discussions with other professionals during adjournments, to relieve tension it is sometimes tempting to adopt a light-hearted, familiar or even humorous tone, but you should never lose sight of the fact that there is likely to be a great deal at stake for some of the people involved and observing too much informality among professionals can cause them confusion or distress, as in Michael's story.

> *At court, parents often get the impression that the social workers are very chummy with the lawyers and all the professionals are in cahoots with each other, which can be bewildering and upsetting.*
>
> (Parents' Aid representative)

> *I know a situation where a solicitor was laughing at serious things.*
>
> (Young person quoted in Ofsted, 2010b, page 24)

In what order do things happen?

All court hearings follow essentially the same pattern. There are basically two types of hearing:

- Hearings in anticipation of a trial.

- The formal trial.

Pre-trial hearings may be the result of a court order that there should be a hearing, or because one of the parties has made an application. Case management conferences, issues-resolution hearings, directions hearings and pre-trial reviews are all intended to ensure that cases proceed with as little delay as possible. Not every case will have all of these types of hearing and often they are managed by the lawyers. However, it is never possible to predict exactly what will happen, and preparation is the key:

> *So I walk into court, sitting there thinking 'Oh my God, I hope they don't ask me any questions' and I was just told 'It's a directions hearing, just go there, sit down and you don't have to say anything', and then I went in and there were all these questions.*
>
> (Social worker quoted by Dickens, 2004b)

Any hearing or trial begins by being called on. For private hearings this simply involves the usher saying that the judge is ready to deal with the case. In open court hearings the clerk or usher announces the case, which alerts everyone that it is about to begin, and records the name of the case on the tape recording made of most hearings in open court. The lawyer for the party who initiated the proceedings then introduces the other lawyers and what happens next depends on whether the hearing is of an application or is a trial.

Applications

An application can be made by any party. In civil and family cases the lawyers usually deliver to court in advance skeleton arguments which set out what the application is about, a summary of the evidence, and the arguments relied upon to support or oppose it. The judge reads these beforehand and may also read the case papers. Sets of the relevant papers are usually copied and assembled in files called bundles, each of which is separately numbered. Often dividers, known as tabs, are inserted to mark sections with documents of a particular type, such as previous court orders. You may therefore hear references to bundle A tab 3, and so on. Bundles are usually sent to court in advance by post or courier and there is a good chance that they will arrive crushed, with the rings out of alignment, which provides considerable scope for displays of judicial dissatisfaction. Another potential source of difficulty is bundles being numbered differently, particularly if the judge's bundles have different page numbers from everyone else's, or if pages have been added after a hearing has started and someone's bundle has been left out of the process.

Applications proceed as follows, unless they are being made without notice and the respondent does not attend, which could happen, for example, in relation to an application for an emergency protection order under s. 44 of the Children Act 1989:

- **Applicant's lawyer opens the application** by explaining what it is about and referring to evidence relied on to support it and any evidence in opposition. As the hearing is not a trial, the evidence consists only of written witness statements and any documents attached. The lawyer then puts forward arguments as to why the application should be granted. If the application is a case management conference or a pre-trial review, it is opened by the claimant's lawyer (or prosecution in a criminal case) who explains what the case is about. It is unlikely that there will be any evidence as the focus is usually practical matters.

- **Lawyers for opposing parties put arguments to the court** Conventionally the respondents' arguments are put by the first respondent, followed by the second respondent and so on, although sometimes groups of respondents use the same lawyer. If some respondents support the application and some oppose it, supporting arguments are heard before the opposing ones.

- **Applicant's lawyer closes the application** by responding to the arguments against it.

- **Judge's decision.**

Civil trials

As we have seen, civil trials tend more towards a *cards on the table* approach than *trial by ambush* (Bond et al., 2007, page 4). The case papers are assembled in the same way as for applications, and they proceed as follows:

- **Claimant's lawyer explains what the case is about (opens the case)** Skeleton arguments are the rule and the judge reads the case papers beforehand. Consequently the opening of the case may be quite short. However, the lawyer may read out, or ask the judge to read, further documents which can take hours, or even days, if the case is complex.

- **Claimant's witnesses give oral evidence** If witness statements are not disputed, they are taken as read and witnesses need only attend court if another party's lawyer wishes to question them. The first witness is usually the claimant. There usually follow other witnesses of fact and then any expert witnesses. However, the order can be adapted to accommodate witnesses with other commitments and avoid keeping people waiting. As we have seen, evidence in chief of witnesses in civil trials is given in writing. The lawyer for the party calling a witness may ask the judge's permission to ask additional questions but this is only granted if there is a valid reason, such as the fact that something in another witness statement needs to be answered and is not covered in the witness's existing statement. If there are no supplementary questions, witnesses are invited to look at their statements, asked whether they have read them recently and whether the contents are true.

- **Cross-examination of claimant's witnesses by lawyers for the other parties** Each witness is cross-examined after verifying their witness statement. This usually takes place in the order in which the parties are listed in the court documents, which is claimant followed by defendants first to last. This order may be adjusted so that cross-examination by lawyers for parties sympathetic to the case of the party calling the witness takes place before cross-examination by parties hostile to the case. This is so that *friendly* cross-examination cannot try to undo any damage done previously by *hostile* cross-examination.

- **Re-examination by claimant's lawyer** This is an opportunity to clarify evidence which may have been based on misunderstanding a question or not being shown a relevant document. However, it can weaken the evidence from the point of view of the party calling the witness because if the evidence which the lawyer thinks is damaging is the witness's true evidence, seeking to undo it but having it confirmed simply draws attention to it. Also, after cross-examination witnesses tend to relax when facing their own lawyer, which can produce lapses in concentration, failure to listen to questions properly and, possibly, unexpected or unfortunate admissions.

- **Claimant's lawyer closes case** After this claimants cannot call further evidence without the court's permission.

- **Defendant's evidence** Defendants can insist that all of the claimant's evidence is heard before any evidence is given on their behalf because they do not have to call any evidence, even if they have served witness statements. However, if a statement or expert's report is served without its author giving evidence, another party can rely on the statement or report as evidence. Unless a defendant is preserving the option not to call evidence, in cases with a strong technical element the factual evidence is sometimes heard before expert evidence, which is sensible if none of the experts knows the facts of the case and there is a serious dispute about them. If the factual evidence is heard first, the experts can take account of this.

- **Cross-examination by other defendants' lawyers, if there are any**

- **Cross-examination by claimant's lawyer, who can rely on any favourable answers in support of their case**

- **Re-examination by defendant's lawyer**

- **Defendant's lawyer closes their case**

- **Closing speeches** are usually made in reverse order to the listing on the formal court documents, so the claimant's lawyer usually has the last word. However, if a defendant has called no evidence, their lawyer is entitled to make the last speech. In closing speeches lawyers make submissions, which means advancing arguments as to what evidence the judge should accept, what the relevant law is, and how it should be applied to the facts of the case.

- **The judge's decision** not only involves deciding who has won, but also what findings of fact to make, determining, if disputed, the relevant law, and applying it to the facts which are found proved. The formal judgement sets out the judge's findings and the reasons for them. Depending upon the length and complexity of the trial, judgement may be given orally at once (called *ex tempore,* Latin for *at the time*) or later, called *reserving judgement*. Unless the delay is no longer than overnight, a reserved judgement is almost always in writing. Written judgements are not read out in court but are provided to the parties and their lawyers in advance. They must not tell anyone the result before the judgement is given formally, a process called *handing down.* Then there are arguments about costs and a formal order, also called, confusingly, a judgement, is prepared to give effect to the decision.

Trials in family cases

These are similar to other civil trials and are usually called final hearings. The lawyers open their case and evidence is called in the same way. The order of proceedings under the Children Act 1989 is determined by Rule 4.21 of the Family Proceedings Rules 1991. Each party explains its case and calls evidence in the following order:

- Applicant.

- Anyone with parental responsibility.

- Other respondents.

- Children's guardian.

- Child, if a party to the proceedings and there is no children's guardian.

PRACTITIONER REFLECTION **8.2**

The first witness often takes the longest, due to the need for each party to impress their case on the court. I suggest that social workers ask their advocate or legal team to ensure that the independent expert gives evidence first rather than the social worker. The expert will crystallise the issues in the case which should prevent the social worker being subjected to unnecessary cross-examination. This aspect of case management usually helps define the issues for the court.

(Family court judge)

Criminal trials

In crown courts defendants usually admit or deny (*plead to*) each charge (*count*) in the list of charges (*indictment*) against them at a plea and case management hearing, when arrangements are also made for the trial if there is a *not guilty* plea to any charge. If a defendant is asked how they plead at the start of what is supposed to be the trial, it is probably because they are changing a previous plea from *not guilty* to *guilty*. In magistrates' courts, pleas are entered before or at the start of the trial.

Criminal trials are conducted rather differently from civil ones:

- **Start of trial** The court is told whether the defendant has admitted or not admitted any of the charges. In magistrates' courts there is no jury and the trial starts once it is clear what charges the defendant faces.

- **Crown court jury is sworn in** *(empanelled)* A group of about fifteen people is brought into court. Their names are written on cards which are shuffled by the court clerk, who calls them out in order from the top, after which those named go to sit in the jury box. Anyone who knows the defendant or someone connected with the case is excused, which is why the number of people brought into court is more than the twelve required. Any objections to potential jurors are dealt with as they come to take the oath *faithfully to try the defendant and to give a true verdict according to the evidence*. Lawyers and judges used to be prohibited from serving on juries but since exemptions were lifted in 2004 jury summoning officers have had a lot of fun calling judges to serve on juries.

- **Prosecution opens its case** The jury is shown the indictment but is unlikely to know if the defendant has admitted any charge unless the defendant requests it. For example, a defendant who admits to having killed someone, but denies that it was intended, may admit manslaughter but deny murder. The burden of proving guilt of a criminal charge is on the prosecution, which describes the charges against the defendant and the evidence to be called to support them. In crown courts, and in limited types of case in magistrates' courts, defendants have to tell the prosecution what their defence is, but do not have to disclose the evidence on which they intend to rely.

- **Prosecution calls its evidence** Unlike in civil proceedings, evidence in chief is given orally, prompted by questions, and leading questions are not permitted. Witnesses therefore have to try to remember what is in their statement, which is particularly challenging if the incident in question occurred some time previously. During the prosecution evidence the jury may be asked to retire for the judge to make a ruling of law. Often the issue relates to the admissibility of evidence under the technical rules which apply in criminal cases. In civil cases more or less any evidence is admissible and it is up to the judge to decide what it is worth, but in criminal cases the rules are intended to ensure that the jury only hears evidence which, if they believe it, would be reliable evidence on which to base a conviction.

- **Cross-examination of prosecution witnesses by defence lawyers** Each of them has a copy of the witness's statement, although the witness does not. Each witness is cross-examined immediately after giving evidence in chief. Defendants who are not legally represented can personally cross-examine prosecution witnesses in most cases.

- **Re-examination by prosecution**

- **Possible submission by defence** At this point the defendant's lawyers can make a submission to the judge or magistrates that the prosecution has not proved its case, even if the defendant calls no evidence *(discloses no case to answer)*. If the submission is accepted, the jury is directed to return a *not guilty* verdict. Submissions take place in the jury's absence so that they are not influenced if the judge rejects them, but magistrates are supposed to be able to proceed uninfluenced by an unsuccessful submission of no case to answer.

- **Evidence from defendant** If the trial is not ended by a successful submission of no case to answer, defendants must decide whether to give evidence themselves. If they choose not to, it will be the subject of comment by the judge before the jury considers its verdict and is also taken into account by magistrates in reaching a decision. A defendant who gives evidence is the first of the defence witnesses to be called. Defendants' evidence is given in the same way as prosecution evidence, by question and answer. The prosecution does not have statements from defendants or their witnesses and so does not usually know what they are likely to say. Defendants with no previous convictions are entitled to call evidence of their good character.

- **Cross-examination of defendant's witnesses** Cross-examination of defence witnesses is by lawyers for any other defendants, in the order on the indictment, and then by the prosecution.

- **Re-examination by defendant's lawyer**

- **Prosecution makes submissions** as to what evidence should be accepted and the law which, on the facts put forward, proves that the defendant is guilty of the alleged charges.

- **Defendants' lawyers make submissions** Defendants' lawyers do not have to try to persuade the jury or the magistrates that their client is innocent, but concentrate on emphasising doubts that they are guilty. They may also make submissions as to which witnesses should be believed, and possibly as to the relevant law.

- **Judge's summing up** In crown courts the judge reminds the jury that he deals with questions of law and they decide the facts. The jury is then instructed on the law which they must apply to the facts, known as *directions to the jury*. The judge also reminds the jury of the evidence which the judge thinks is important, but this is not binding on jurors who can make their own decisions about both evidence and facts.

- **Court considers its verdict** Most judges do not send a jury out to consider a verdict after about 3 p.m. They adjourn the case and leave about five minutes' worth of summing up for the following morning. If the jury reaches unanimous agreement, they return to announce their verdict. If they cannot agree within about two and a quarter hours, the judge asks whether they are likely to be able to reach a unanimous verdict, in which case they continue their deliberations. If they indicate this is unlikely, the judge tells them that a verdict on which at least ten of them agree can be accepted and they continue their discussions which, in long and complex cases, can last days. However, usually, after a few hours the judge says that the court will take any verdicts which have been agreed and discharges the jury from reaching verdicts on any counts on which they cannot agree. If guilty verdicts are returned, the question of sentence arises. After the speeches for the defendants, magistrates decide whether the case against them has been proved.

- **Sentencing** There are restrictions on courts imposing a term of imprisonment without first obtaining a pre-sentence report from the probation or youth offending service. Whether a community sentence is appropriate is also a decision which can usually only be made after the court knows what is available. Consequently, after a *guilty* verdict most cases are adjourned for reports, although occasionally a *stand-down report* is requested, which is undertaken by a probation officer or youth justice worker on the spot. The sentencing part of a hearing follows much the same format, whether or not it has been adjourned previously. The prosecution details the defendant's criminal record, if there is one. If it is long, the court may ask that only the last X offences, or a summary, are given. If the defendant has no previous convictions, details of their family circumstances and employment are given. The defendant's lawyer then makes a *plea in mitigation,* a speech about the appropriate punishment which takes account of information or recommendations in any reports and any previous convictions. More details of the defendant's circumstances and plans are usually given, together with expressions of remorse, unless this is totally implausible. The judge or magistrates announce the sentence and explain aspects of the sentencing decision and its effects. In serious cases, reference to protection of the public and the impact on any victim may be included, which can take account of any *victim impact statement* which may have been presented to the court.

France In serious criminal cases a jury of nine retires with the three judges and all decide together on the defendant's guilt and the sentence to be applied.

Germany There is no jury as such and prosecutions potentially leading to a maximum sentence of one year's imprisonment are heard by a single judge. More serious cases are decided by a judge sitting with two lay (unqualified) judges, and cases in which the possible sentence exceeds three years' imprisonment are referred to a *Land* court where they are heard by a combination of professional and lay judges.

Scotland The jury numbers 15 and there is a third verdict in addition to *guilty* and *not guilty*, of *not proven*, which is similar in effect to a *not guilty* verdict, but indicates that the jury was not particularly impressed by the defence case.

France, Spain and Russia The jury is asked to provide answers to questions formulated by the judge – in other words, they have to show how they have reached their verdict.

Figure 8.5 *Alternative types of criminal trial*

ACTIVITY 8.4

This exercise encourages you to think critically about procedures which apply in criminal courts, particularly from the point of view of defendants.

Juries' discussions are secret and they are not required to give reasons for their decisions. Also, juries have no role in relation to sentencing if they find someone guilty.

- *Do you think this is compatible with Article 6 of the European Convention on Human Rights (right to a fair trial)?*
- *Do you think a jury trial is a fair method of determining guilt?*
- *What alternative system could you suggest?*

Recording the proceedings

In all courts someone records what is said, even if it is only the judge in a notebook. These notes are for the judge's own use and, as the judge is unlikely to have shorthand skills, they will not be verbatim notes. In civil and family proceedings, because the evidence in chief is in writing, the judge notes the important parts of the evidence which supplement the witness statements and that given in cross-examination and re-examination. In crown court trials, judges make a note of verbal evidence from prosecution witnesses, even though they have copies of the witness statements, because what is said in court may be different from what is contained in the statements. Defence witnesses' evidence in chief will be noted, but not usually evidence of police interviews because these are taped and usually an agreed written summary, or extracts, are put to the jury.

All High Court hearings are tape-recorded; the microphones are not for amplification but for recording. In crown courts a verbatim record is made, either by tape-recording or by a stenographer. Some county court proceedings are taped, although hearings in district judge's private rooms often are not. In magistrates' courts the clerk makes a note of the evidence.

Reporting the proceedings

The Press can attend any hearing which is not private, which includes hearings in magistrates' courts, including youth and family courts. They can also attend crown, county and High Court hearings. The Press can report anything that is said other than in private, including the evidence of witnesses. Most reporters are not specialists, so reports of anything remotely technical are unlikely to be more than partially accurate and in any event only perceived highlights are picked out, which may give a distorted representation of the case. In relation to the recently lifted restriction on reporting family cases, the Press appears to have shown little interest in reporting on the difficult and sometimes controversial decisions which have to be made (Ministry of Justice, 2010a).

As we have seen, an important element of English law is precedent, that is, decisions in other cases. Decisions on new points of law need to be disseminated and so professional law reporters decide whether judgements, usually only those of the High Court, Court of Appeal or Supreme Court, are worth reporting. Specialist law reports are published periodically, like magazines.

ACTIVITY 8.5

Law reports appear in The Times *on most days when the High Court is sitting. Other newspapers usually publish them weekly and they are available on various websites (see below). They will give you a flavour of legal decision-making and it may be helpful to keep cuttings which relate to decisions in cases within your area of interest.*

Practical arrangements

Part of preparing for court involves making practical arrangements to enable you to attend the hearing without being distracted by other concerns. The first essential is to establish how long it is likely to last. In a family case you are likely to be required throughout the hearing and so you should ensure that you do not have any conflicting professional or personal obligations. Most court hearings do not begin before 10.30 a.m. or continue after 4.30 p.m. However, magistrates and district judges sometimes operate outside these hours in order to finish a case.

The next example demonstrates the importance of anticipating the possibility of unexpected events, and ensuring that adequate support is on hand when making practical arrangements:

CASE STUDY 8.1

In care proceedings being heard in a magistrates' court, the local authority was represented by a private solicitor and a legal executive from the authority's legal department. The magistrates sat beyond the expected finish time in order to complete the hearing, which finally ended around 7 p.m. The decision not to make a care order was completely unexpected, which left the social worker without any support or effective legal advice about what to do next. While attempts were made to contact managers and a lawyer in the legal department, all the social worker could do was alert the foster carers that the parents were coming to collect the child.

Finding the court building

You are probably aware of the location and layout of your local courts, and information about every court in the country can be found on the website of HM Courts and Tribunals Service. Crown and magistrates' courts usually have a building to themselves, or at least share only with other courts. Some county courts share a building with other courts, but others are situated in an office block with other businesses or organisations. Always leave plenty of time to allow for normal travelling hazards, parking and two additional potential sources of delay, security and finding the court once you reach the building. Arriving late and flustered is not recommended.

Security

Courts, like many public buildings, are regarded as potential terrorist targets and airport-style security exists in all crown courts and in the Royal Courts of Justice. In magistrates' and county courts you may also have your bags searched, pass through a metal detector or be subjected to a body search. You will reduce delay if you ensure that anything likely to trigger the metal detector, such as mobile phone, keys or loose change, is in your bag and not in your pocket. Court staff and judges all have security clearance and use different entrances from the general public. Lawyers, however, are subject to the same security procedures as anyone else.

Finding the right court

The challenge of this task should not be underestimated as it is unlikely that there is a court in the country with only one courtroom. A building accommodating only magistrates' courts typically has up to four courtrooms, while a purpose-built crown court may have up to eight. A county court in an office block usually has two courtrooms and several rooms used by district judges, which are likely to have a separate waiting area. Combined Court Centres, containing both crown and county courts, may also include magistrates' courts, with the courtrooms used for whatever cases are being heard on the day. In one court the crown court could be trying a murder case while next door there could be a county court hearing.

If your hearing is before a district judge in a county court, or a Master or a Registrar in the High Court, it will take place in the judge's private room, and the notice of the hearing may say which that is. For some open court hearings it is possible to find out on the afternoon of the previous day where the hearing will take place. In the High Court a case list is published each afternoon on the HM Courts and Tribunals Service website in respect of the following day's sittings, and a comprehensive list of all court hearings other than in magistrates' courts can be accessed by your legal advisers via various subscription websites. The designated court may change at any time before the hearing, so you need to check again when you arrive.

After passing through security, you may find a board listing the day's cases, and there are usually signs in the larger courts indicating where each courtroom is located. However, if there is no list you will have to ask. In magistrates' courts, and for county court hearings before district judges, an usher will probably be in the waiting area noting who has arrived for which case. For hearings in open court this is less likely, but the security personnel should be able to show you where to go. If the hearing is in a private room, you are not expected to enter until your hearing starts. If the hearing is in a courtroom, you could go and sit at the back, if the court is open. Some courtrooms are only unlocked just before the start of each hearing.

What to wear

The guiding rule is that your clothing should not draw more attention to your appearance than to your evidence. You do not have to wear a suit, but you should dress in a way which is consistent with your professional status. For women, there is no need to wear a skirt or dress rather than trousers, or a dark colour if you would be happier in something brighter. Most courts, however, expect men to wear a jacket, shirt and tie rather than a sweater or T-shirt. Within reason, they can be any colour or pattern.

What not to wear

- Jeans – ever.

- Anything tight, short or revealing.

- Anything in which you will not be comfortable sitting for a whole day.

- Anything which might reinforce the stereotype of a social worker, like a flowing print skirt, long dangling earrings or open-toed sandals.

PRACTITIONER REFLECTION 8.3

I once saw a young social worker come to court carrying a bright pink handbag. You might think that this was irrelevant, but there are unwritten rules about how to present yourself professionally in court and you need to take account of them if you want to fit in. You are very quickly judged if you don't seem to know the ropes.

(CAFCASS manager)

Another point to note is that if you are attending court with your client, whether or not there is an issue of conflict between you, it is likely to reinforce your client's anxiety and apprehension and increase their perception of the power differential between you if your court clothes are very different from what you usually wear for work.

*NLINE
ESOURCES*

www.lawreports.co.uk

The Incorporated Council of Law Reporting provides free access to legal case summaries.

www.bailii.org.uk

British and Irish Legal Information Institute provides access to public legal information, including recent cases and current legislation.

www.hmcourts-service.gov.uk/HMCSCourtFinder

This website has information about every court in the country, including photograph, opening hours, types of case dealt with and contact details for administrative staff.

Chapter 9
Giving evidence

This chapter will help you to meet the following National Occupational Standards for social work.

- Key role 5: Manage and be accountable, with supervision and support, for your own social work practice within your organisation.
  - Carry out duties using accountable professional judgement and knowledge-based social work practice.
  - Provide evidence for judgements and decisions.

- Key role 6: Demonstrate professional competence in social work practice.
  - Review and update your own knowledge of legal, policy and procedural frameworks.
  - Exercise and justify professional judgements.
  - Use professional assertiveness to justify decisions and uphold professional social work practice, values and ethics.

Introduction

In this chapter we look at the mechanics of giving evidence. We have already explained that, unless you are a witness of fact in criminal proceedings, your main evidence, the *evidence in chief*, is presented in a written statement. How to deal with cross-examination on your evidence is considered in Chapter 10. We also consider the support and protection available to vulnerable witnesses.

PRACTITIONER REFLECTION 9.1

The social worker is likely to be the only witness before the court who really knows the parents' strengths and weaknesses. It is important for social workers to be fair to the parents so that the court is able to rely on measured and well-balanced evidence.

(Family court judge)

If you've been working hard to improve things in a family, it's not easy to shift from being the helpful, supportive social worker to one who is having to take a forensic view of all aspects of the case.

(CAFCASS team manager)

Social workers' status as witness

The case of *F* v. *Suffolk County Council* [1981] 2 FLR 208 established that social workers can be regarded by courts as experts in child care issues. However, they do not have expertise in relation to the diagnosis of sexual abuse (*Re N.* [1996] 2 FLR 2), nor in relation to whether children's evidence can be accepted.

Expert witness	Lawyer
Independent	Partisan
Neutral	Puts client's case
Knows field, not law	Knows law, not field
Never argues	Argues if necessary
Assists court	Persuades court
Not a 'hired gun'	Paid by, or on behalf of, client
Can coach lawyer	Cannot coach expert

Figure 9.1 *Contrasting roles of expert witness and lawyer (Bond et al., 2007, page 62)*

You may find it surprising, in view of the emphasis on collaborative and interdisciplinary working, that in court you do not give evidence as a member of a team, but as an individual. As an employee, you obviously follow the instructions of your managers; if, for example, it is decided to initiate care proceedings and you are instructed to take this forward, then you must do this. However, once in court your primary duty is to the court, which requires you to give evidence of your personal knowledge and opinions, not those of anyone else. You do not have to support the line of the party on whose behalf you are giving evidence if, on professional grounds, you do not. This can be difficult, particularly if you are relatively inexperienced, but it is important. If the court wishes to hear from your team or service manager or anyone else, then they can be called to give evidence, and indeed should be if their views and decisions are important to the case.

Must you give evidence?

In most cases, the answer is yes. Anyone can be required to attend court if their evidence is considered relevant and if you are the case social worker in care proceedings your evidence will be relevant. You are also not likely to be entitled to anonymity, even if you are apprehensive about possible consequences, as made clear in *Re W (Children) (Care Proceedings: Witness Anonymity)* [2002] EWCA Civ 1626 when the Court of Appeal said: *Cases in which the court will afford anonymity to a professional social work witness will be highly exceptional.*

Exposure of witnesses to liability as a result of giving evidence

You may be concerned as to what extent you may be exposed as a result of giving evidence and, in particular whether, if the case for the party on whose behalf you are appearing is unsuccessful, you could be sued for libel or slander. (Libel is defamatory material in a document; slander is defamation by spoken word.) Occasionally people have tried to retaliate against witnesses who have spoken against them, and so you will be relieved to know that the rules are clear. Essentially you have nothing to fear, unless what you say is untrue.

In criminal proceedings, unless statements are made which are unrelated to the prosecution, witnesses are totally immune from being sued. In civil proceedings witnesses have absolute privilege against exposure to defamation, and witness statements cannot be used for any purpose other than the proceedings in which they are served, unless the witness consents, the court gives permission, or the statement has been put in evidence at a public hearing. Consequently, if someone discovers the content of a witness statement, which is not in fact put forward in evidence, they cannot rely on it, for example in support of a claim for defamation, without either the consent of the witness (who will not give it) or the court, which would be very unlikely to give permission solely to enable an aggrieved person to sue.

Witness preparation

In England and Wales this is a sensitive subject. In the United States it is common for witnesses to be coached on how to give evidence, which involves mock cross-examination on the actual facts and issues in the case, and suggestions as to how particular questions should be answered. The whole exercise is designed to manipulate the witness's evidence so as to make it as favourable as possible. In England and Wales this is absolutely forbidden. What is permitted is one of the objects of this book, to familiarise witnesses with the layout of a court, the likely sequence of events at a hearing and the different roles and responsibilities of the various participants. The Bar Council (2005) has produced guidance on witness preparation:

> *4. ... Such arrangements* [that is, the familiarisation process just described] *prevent witnesses from being disadvantaged by ignorance of the process or being taken by surprise at the way in which it works, and so assist witnesses to give of their best ..., without any risk that their evidence may become anything other than the witnesses' own uncontaminated evidence....*

> *5. ... it is also appropriate, as part of a witness familiarisation process, for barristers to advise witnesses as to the basic requirements for giving evidence, e.g. the need to listen to and answer the question put, to speak clearly and slowly in order to ensure that the court hears what the witness is saying, and to avoid irrelevant comments....*

This guidance applies to you in two ways:

- You should not expect to be coached in your evidence and if coaching is offered, you should refuse to have anything to do with it.

- You should not discuss with potential witnesses what their evidence will be or how they should answer particular questions. This does not mean that you cannot discuss the case or the issues in it, which would make your job impossible in any case which was likely to go to court. The important thing is to avoid making any suggestions about what the evidence should be, or how it should be given.

Hearsay

Hearsay is evidence of what someone has told you, rather than evidence of what you saw, heard, smelled, touched or tasted yourself. If it is relevant to know what someone said to you, as opposed to whether what they said was accurate, evidence of this is not hearsay. If a child tells you that they are being bullied at school, it is evidence of what they told you, but not evidence of the fact that they are being bullied. The rules of hearsay are important in criminal cases, but less so in civil cases, and rules made under the Children Act 1989 give courts the power to allow hearsay evidence in cases involving the welfare of children. However, courts always seek the best available evidence, which means that they should not be offered second-hand evidence if first-hand evidence is available in relation to the matter in question.

CASE STUDY 9.1

In a case where one of the matters at issue was the likelihood of a family being allocated council housing, and the social worker had included in her witness statement details of the housing department's position as set out in correspondence, the court ordered the housing manager to give evidence. Perhaps unsurprisingly, the manager presented to the court a more optimistic view than that provided previously to the social worker. This example shows how careful you must be when representing the views of anyone else.

The legal rules governing what can be said in evidence can be quite complicated. However, you do not need to worry about them, even if you are giving evidence in a criminal case. If the lawyers think that your answers are inadmissible as evidence, it is for them or the judge to deal with it.

Preparation for giving evidence in chief

It is important to reread your witness statement before you give evidence. In civil cases you do not have to try to remember everything because your statement is available to you as you give evidence. However, you do have to confirm that it is true, so you should check it carefully. Note any errors and ensure that they are corrected. Failure to detect errors looks unprofessional and may cast doubt on the quality of your evidence. If, when asked whether you have read your statement recently, you say *no*, you will probably have to sit and read it in court, which may embarrass you and make the process of giving evidence more difficult. It may also mean that in your anxiety to get to the end, you will not read it sufficiently carefully.

What to do while waiting to give evidence

Court proceedings take much longer than you might imagine. Any case other than the most straightforward will last hours, or possibly days, and so if you are a witness in a criminal trial, or supporting someone who is, bring plenty to read while you are waiting. Witnesses of fact in criminal trials must not have contact with the defendant or lawyers acting for anyone other than the person on whose behalf they are giving evidence. If you are in court while waiting to give evidence in a family case, you may need to communicate with the lawyers for the party for whom you are being called as a witness. However, whispering and passing notes is not only distracting, but could be interpreted by others as being over-partisan.

When to enter the witness box

Television films tend to give the impression that when it is time for you to give evidence, someone in court will shout out, *Call,* [your name], which is echoed by a number of officials until the message reaches you. In practice this is not what happens at all.

In civil or family proceedings you are normally present in court when it is time for you to give evidence. Occasionally witnesses are asked to wait outside the courtroom, but it is unusual. In criminal proceedings it is different, because it is thought important that witnesses do not hear other witnesses' evidence until they have completed their own. Therefore, if you are a witness of fact in a criminal trial, you will be told where to wait and when you are required.

How to enter the witness box

This might seem a strange thing to comment on, but some judges do not like it if your path to the witness box takes you between the lawyers and the judge. Choose a route which takes you from wherever you are sitting or entering the court, round the back of the rows of lawyers, to the witness box. Move calmly and try not to rush or drop anything which you are taking with you.

What to take with you into the witness box

There are no cloakrooms at courts, so if you are wearing a coat or carrying a briefcase you must bring them with you into the courtroom. You should not, however, take them into the witness box; they can be left on or under a seat in the public part of the court. If you are the main representative of the local authority in the case, you may be asked to sit next to the solicitor acting for the authority, so that the barrister who sits in front can talk to you during the hearing, a process called *taking instructions*. If you are sitting next to the solicitor, you can leave your belongings there. You can take your handbag with you, but space in the witness box is limited and so it is best to put it on the floor beside it. Remember to take anything you may need as an aid to giving evidence, such as your glasses.

Usually a set of the bundles of documents in the case is placed in the witness box before you come to give evidence. These should include a copy of your witness statement and copies of documents to which you may be asked to refer. You need not, therefore, take with you your witness statement or the case file unless specifically asked to do so. You should, however, know where your file is in court, in case you need to refer to it. You should never take into the witness box any notes which you may have made for your own use, like comments on the witness statements of others. If you do, you will probably find your private thoughts being shared with everyone present.

The oath

When you arrive in the witness box you should stay standing. Before giving evidence, witnesses must either take an oath or affirm. It is your choice and you have a right to affirm if you wish. If you take the oath, you should be asked on which holy book you wish to take it.

That's the theory.

In practice you will probably find the usher asking, *What religion are you?* and assuming that you will swear on the holy book of that religion, if there is a copy in court. Courts often do not have even the holy books of the principal religions represented in this country today. If the usher cannot immediately find the relevant book, it may be suggested that you swear on the New Testament. However, if there is a copy in the building of the book on which you wish to swear, reasonable efforts should be made to obtain it for you. If it is not available, you can be required to affirm. The affirmation of a witness is, *I do solemnly, sincerely and truly declare and affirm that the evidence I shall give shall be the truth, the whole truth and nothing but the truth.*

If your religion requires any preliminaries to be completed before taking an oath, such as washing, you should have an opportunity to carry them out. Holy books of religions which prohibit the handling of scripture other than by the ritually pure are usually kept in a cloth cover and if you wish to swear on such a book it should be handed to you in its cover. You should remove it from the cover and replace it after taking the oath.

The oath taken by a witness who is a Christian is, *I swear by Almighty God that the evidence I shall give shall be the truth, the whole truth and nothing but the truth*. Christians swear on the New Testament. If taken by a member of another religion the words *Almighty God* are replaced with the name of the appropriate designation of God, such as *Allah*, or, if it is the custom to swear by the book itself, the name of the book, as in *I swear by the Bhagavad Gita.*

The taking of the oath or the making of an affirmation is important to the person concerned as it is a solemn promise to tell the truth, and it is also an important part of the judicial process. An affirmation has the same force and effect as an oath; if you tell lies under oath or having affirmed, you can be prosecuted for perjury. There should be silence while the oath is being taken or an affirmation made. The book on which the oath is taken should be held in a raised hand. This does not have to be the right hand, although you would not think so from the number of times the person administering the oath says *take the book in your right hand.*

What happens if you swear on the wrong book or stumble over the words? What's important is that the person taking the oath considers it to be binding, even if the wrong words or book are used. In *R v. Kemble* [1990] 91 Cr. App. R. 178, a Muslim witness swore on the New Testament. He said that he considered an oath sworn on any holy book was binding on his conscience and his oath was held to be valid. You don't get off the hook if you do not believe in the religion on whose holy book you have sworn – the oath is still valid.

Children under 14 are not permitted to take the oath before giving evidence in criminal trials (Youth Justice and Criminal Evidence Act, 1999, s.55).

Sit or stand?

Witnesses in civil trials or family hearings are usually allowed to sit. A good rule of thumb is that if a chair is provided, it is there to be used. However, some judges prefer witnesses to ask if they may sit before doing so. Just because there is a chair does not mean that you have to use it. It is difficult to feel relaxed in a chair without arms or when the height of the witness box interferes with your view of the courtroom. You may be more comfortable standing as it is easier to reach the witness bundles and to breathe more slowly, which will help calm your nerves. You may also feel more in control, as the lawyer questioning you will also be standing. If you stand, your body language may be more obvious to others in the court, but as we discuss below, this is likely to be of more concern to you than anyone else. If you are very nervous and feel shaky, hold on to the edge of the witness box or the chair. In criminal trials witnesses normally stand while giving evidence and often no chair is provided. If you need a chair, ask for one, but you may be asked why you want to sit. Surprisingly, you may find that *I have been standing giving evidence for two hours and I am tired* is not always considered sufficient.

Volume and speed

It is important to be prepared for how loudly you need to speak in court, and at what speed. If there are microphones, they are not for amplification but to record the proceedings. It is essential that your evidence is heard by the magistrates or judge, the jury, if there is one, and all of the lawyers. If any of these cannot hear you, you will be asked to speak up, which can be off-putting if you are nervous, and if it happens several times there is a risk that the judge will become irritated. Before you give evidence, try to assess other speakers in court, so that you have an idea of how loudly you will need to speak, but don't shout. You will be fascinated to know that judges have hearing tests on appointment and do not need to be harangued as if they were at a public meeting.

ACTIVITY **9.1**

- *Observe people presenting their views, or answering questions, in a variety of settings (television debate, church service, play, lecture, party political broadcast).*

- *Note what seems to support effective communication in terms of volume and speed, and what creates barriers between speaker and listener.*

This activity shows that you can improve your presentation skills by careful observation in the course of everyday activities.

Many witnesses speak too fast, usually because of nervousness, and it is sensible to practise speaking more slowly as this will give you additional thinking time as well as assisting those who have to listen to, and make a note of, your evidence. You may be advised by a lawyer to *follow his Lordship's pen,* which is supposed to encourage you to speak at dictation speed so that the judge can write everything down. However, while judges do make a note of the evidence, they do not need to record every single word. A judge who is finding it difficult to keep up will certainly say so. Don't be distracted from concentrating on answering the questions by trying to look in a direction in which you would not otherwise be looking. Watching the speed at which judges write is about as interesting as watching grass grow. Usually, when lawyers tell you to *follow his Lordship's pen*, they are really telling the judge to make a careful note of the evidence. Some lawyers manage, perhaps inadvertently, to distract witnesses and make their task more difficult by saying something like, *I shall be asking the questions, but direct your answers to his Lordship/the magistrates.* If you complied with this instruction you would be twisting round every time you were asked a question. What is important is that your answers are heard by everyone. It is not easy to make a note of what is being said while looking at a witness, so the judge is likely to be concentrating on taking notes rather than looking at you.

Verbal additions to your witness statement

When you have taken the oath or affirmed, you have promised to tell *the whole truth*. Does anyone really want to hear it? The answer is probably *no*. However, you may wish to add to your witness statement, perhaps because of a further thought, as a comment on another witness statement, because you have been reminded of something or because something significant has happened since you wrote it. If so, you should tell the lawyer acting for the party on whose behalf you are giving evidence. They can then advise whether you should mention it and, if so, give you the opportunity at the start of your evidence. However, if the lawyer does not think that the matter is worth mentioning and you do, or the lawyer forgets to give you the opportunity, you should raise it before you confirm the accuracy of your witness statement, if it affects something in that statement, or before your cross-examination begins if it is something new. After all, the evidence is yours, not the lawyer's, and no one should prevent you from telling the story in the way that you wish.

We deal with points which occur to you while you are being cross-examined in the next chapter.

Body language

Body language tends to be of more interest to social workers than it is to lawyers. The judge is likely to be too busy making notes to pay much attention to how you sit or whether you fiddle with your glasses, and lawyers are not trained to interpret body language as are social workers. If you do have mannerisms which suggest that you are feeling uncomfortable or nervous, judges are unlikely to attach much significance to them, even if they notice them. For judges and lawyers, courts are part of their normal work environment but many witnesses will never achieve that level of familiarity with them. Courts generally understand and take account of that, and no one will be particularly surprised if you appear anxious. What your body language may convey to others in court is also not likely to be significant. Anyone else is really just a spectator and they may well be sympathetic to you in what they recognise as an ordeal. It is, however, sensible to be aware of the possibility of any negative feelings being leaked through non-verbal means (see example in Chapter 10) and to make use of relaxation techniques you have found helpful in the past.

Relevance

It is not for you to decide whether any of the questions which you are asked are relevant. If any of the lawyers, or the judge, think that a question has been asked the answer to which would be irrelevant, they will say so. Broadly, what is relevant is factual evidence, your analysis and opinions, evidence of your reliability as a witness and evidence of your qualifications to express the opinions which you have, which can include evidence as to the quality of your memory, hearing, eyesight and propensity to be truthful, fair and honest.

Interruptions in the evidence

Unless your evidence is very short, it is likely to be interrupted by an adjournment at the middle or end of the day. Even in civil or family cases, if there is an adjournment during your evidence you should not discuss it, or any issues in the case, with anyone. Sometimes witnesses are reminded of this rule and sometimes they are not. The reason for it is that your evidence should be your own, uninfluenced by anything that anyone else may say to you. If you were to talk to someone about your evidence, they might say *Why did you not mention x?* or *Why did you have to say that?*, which could affect how you give the rest of your evidence. Barristers are prohibited by their professional rules from having contact about the case with witnesses until their evidence has finished without the consent of the lawyers for the other parties or the court, and you should observe the same rule. You can certainly say, *Good morning*, or talk about matters other than the case, but it avoids misunderstanding if you do not speak to them at all, unless loudly enough for the other parties to hear what you are saying. However, this can make you feel very isolated and unsupported if you are giving lengthy evidence in a complex case.

Changes and additions during the course of giving evidence

Inevitably you will reflect on your evidence during adjournments, which may result in you remembering something you should have said, or perhaps being concerned that something you did say has been misunderstood or even inaccurately presented. If this happens, you should raise it when you return to the witness box. However, a note of caution: too dramatic a change in your evidence after a break may suggest that you have been nobbled by someone during the adjournment.

Relations with other parties

Although litigation is an adversarial process, it does not have to be conducted in a hostile way, and much depends on the nature of the case and the personalities of those involved. There is no rule which prevents barristers from exchanging pleasantries with another party's witnesses, but they should not discuss details of the case or the evidence. Barristers and solicitors should be courteous in all their professional dealings, but inevitably you will warm to some more than others. However, stereotypical assumptions about the legal profession can impede effective working relationships (see Activity 4.1 in Chapter 4).

---

*PRACTITIONER REFLECTION **9.2***

It is really difficult knowing what to say to the family when you arrive at court. You don't know whether to say 'Hello', knowing you might be ignored or appear patronising, or collude with the adversarial atmosphere by saying nothing.

(Social worker)

When you arrive at court, find out if your service users are there, go up to them, say 'Good morning', ask how they are and tell them what you are going to do.

(CAFCASS manager)

In family cases involving children, confrontation should be avoided as far as possible and so, although it may be difficult because of the nature of the issues at stake, everyone should try to achieve an atmosphere which is as least tense as possible. If you are involved in a case in which an order is sought against your client, you are probably going to have to continue to work with that client (unlike the lawyers), so there is no point doing anything other than trying to maintain civilised professional relationships. However, it would not be surprising if they wanted to have as little as possible to do with you. Unless you have personal experience of what they are facing, you cannot begin to understand what they are feeling and it would be patronising to suggest that you do. It can be very difficult if you become the focus of hostility when you are only doing your job, but in distressing circumstances it is not uncommon to look for someone to bear the brunt of strong feelings and you should always be sensitive towards those for whom a great deal may be at stake.

ACTIVITY 9.2

It's very satisfying (court work) ... you can't get a better high than coming out of there and saying 'result'!

(Social worker, quoted in Beckett et al., 2007)

I think you need to see the court, the barristers and the guardian and all the representatives, as the enemy and go for it ... and therefore what will happen is that word will be out on the street, so when they get (an authority x case) they go 'Oh no' – that is what I want.

(Social services manager, quoted in Dickens, 2006)

I like the fight.

(Social worker, quoted in Beckett et al., 2007)

- *Do you think these reactions to court experiences are understandable?*
- *Do they accord with social work values and professional codes of practice?*
- *What effect might they have on subsequent relationships with service users?*
- *How might they impact on social workers' future professional development?*

This activity encourages you to think about the effect on your professional performance of allowing yourself to become caught up in the adversarial process.

ACTIVITY 9.3

A study of judicial decision-making and the management of care proceedings (Iweniec et al., 2004) found that once experts' reports were initiated, courts were reluctant to accept social workers as both 'prosecutors' and objective witnesses.

- *What actions on the part of the social worker would help address this?*

This activity encourages you to think creatively about the dilemmas presented by your sometimes conflicting roles at court. It requires you to analyse your professional responsibilities and, drawing on what we have said about fairness and impartiality, consider how you can encourage lawyers, judges and service users to have confidence in your professional objectivity.

Evidence of children and vulnerable adults

As a social worker you may be involved in supporting someone who needs to be a witness in court, and consequently you need to know what special provisions can be made and in what circumstances. The Youth Justice and Criminal Evidence Act 1999 introduced a number of special measures which may be made available to witnesses, in criminal proceedings only, who satisfy the following criteria:

- Are not the accused person in the case.

- Are under 17. Or

- Have a mental disorder or significant impairment of intelligence and social functioning which the court considers likely to affect the quality of their evidence. Or

- Have a physical disorder or disability which the court considers likely to affect the quality of their evidence. Or

- Are a person, the quality of whose evidence the court considers is likely to be diminished by fear or distress. A complainant in a case involving a possible sexual offence automatically fulfils this condition, but does not have to take advantage of it.

The special measures which can be taken include:

- Screens to prevent the witness and accused person seeing each other, although they must not prevent the witness being seen by the judge, jury and lawyers.

- Taking evidence in private, but obviously in the presence of the judge and jury or magistrates, the accused and the lawyers.

- Removal of wigs and robes by the judge and lawyers.

- Giving some, or all, of the evidence by means of a live or pre-recorded video link, if necessary at a different venue.

- Use of an intermediary to convey questions and answers (which could be a social worker).

- Use of a device to enable the witness to receive questions and communicate answers.

A further element of witness protection is that an unrepresented person accused of a sexual offence may not personally cross-examine the alleged victim. A lawyer representing someone in these circumstances may not cross-examine the complainant about previous sexual history without the court's permission, which can only be given on limited grounds.

In deciding whether special measures should be provided, the court must take into account the views of the witness concerned and consider whether the proposed measures are likely to improve the quality of the evidence or, conversely, inhibit evidence being effectively given. Whatever is decided, judges and magistrates are expected to take an active role in minimising the effects of aspects of the court process likely to cause distress (s.6.9, CJS, 2007). Nevertheless, the effectiveness of provision varies:

> *I didn't like the TV link room. I had to sit on 2 cushions and I wasn't allowed to take my toy in.*

> *I was told there was no TV link available but I said I wouldn't do it if I had to go into court so we all moved to another court that had a TV link. It wasn't the least bit organised – the Brownies could have done better.*

> *The judge said, 'One question at a time, please rephrase'. He did this even when I hadn't said I was having a problem. The judge was really excellent.*

> (Young witnesses quoted by Plotnikoff and Woolfson, 2009)

149

In civil and family proceedings, no formal measures exist to assist vulnerable witnesses. As written statements from any witness can be put in evidence, children and vulnerable adults would not normally need to give oral evidence. If it is considered important that a vulnerable witness be cross-examined on their written evidence, the court can take steps to facilitate this and minimise the stress on them. If cross-examination is not possible, it could be the subject of comment in the context of the value (*weight*) of the evidence.

RESEARCH SUMMARY

Children can achieve 80–90% recall when questioned in a supportive manner and in a relaxed environment fairly soon after an event (Westcott, 2006). Other factors found to promote accuracy include:

- *Use of open questions.*

- *Avoidance of jargon and complex language.*

- *Clarification of expectations.*

- *A friendly manner and good non-verbal communication, including eye contact, on the part of the questioner.*

A comprehensive evaluation of the experiences of child witnesses, their parents and managers of witness support schemes (Plotnikoff and Woolfson, 2009) identified a significant gap between policy and practice, particularly in relation to:

- *Visually recorded statements.*

- *Assistance before trial.*

- *Waiting times.*

- *Standards of questioning at court.*

- *Emotional support for young witnesses while giving evidence.*

The study contains detailed comments from child witnesses and their families about their experiences of attending criminal courts.

FURTHER READING

Achieving best evidence in criminal proceedings (CJS, 2007) is advisory and therefore is not legally enforceable.

Children and young people: Crown Prosecution Service policy on prosecuting criminal cases involving children and young people as victims and witnesses (CPS, 2006).

Code of Practice for victims of crime (CJS, 2006) sets out victims' rights and agency obligations contained within the Domestic Violence, Crimes and Victims Act 2004.

The Witness Charter (CJS, 2008) consolidates existing witness commitments and procedures into one document. Unlike the victims' code above, it is not set out in law.

ONLINE
RESOURCES

All CJS publications listed above are available on **www.cjsonline.gov.uk**

www.cjsonline.gov.uk

The Office for Criminal Justice Reform offers support to people involved in the criminal justice system. It manages a register of qualified intermediaries to support witnesses and victims and provides preparatory materials, such as virtual court tours.

www.moj.coionline.tv/videos/goingtocourtvideo/

Offers a step-by-step guide to being a witness, also available as a DVD.

www.nspcc.org.uk

The NSPCC publishes preparatory materials, such as videos and board games, to help prepare children for giving evidence.

www.victimsupport.org.uk

Victim Support's witness service operates in every crown court to offer support to witnesses, victims, their family and friends. It is free and confidential, and normally contacts potential witnesses in advance of any court hearing.

Chapter 10
Cross-examination

This chapter will help you to meet the following National Occupational Standards for social work.

- Key role 5: Manage and be accountable, with supervision and support, for your own social work practice within your organisation.
  - Carry out duties using accountable professional judgement and knowledge-based social work practice.
  - Provide evidence for judgements and decisions.

- Key role 6: Demonstrate professional competence in social work practice.
  - Exercise and justify professional judgements.
  - Use professional assertiveness to justify decisions and uphold professional social work practice, values and ethics.

Introduction

Cross-examination takes place in both criminal and civil proceedings and is the part of the trial process which is usually most daunting to witnesses. Even the term *cross-examination* may be intimidating, suggesting a hostile experience in the course of which the questioner becomes *cross*. This is misleading, since the process need not be, and often is not, hostile, particularly in family proceedings. However, it is never likely to be particularly pleasant, not least because the anticipation of an ordeal often contributes as much, if not more, stress than the experience itself.

If you are not used to giving evidence it is easy to imagine that all sorts of terrors lie in wait once you enter the witness box to be cross-examined.

- Will the judge be sympathetic or intimidating?

- Will the advocates make me look foolish or ignorant?

- Will they try to bully me, or trick me into saying things that I do not mean?

- What happens if I forget something important or become confused?

These natural fears may stem from anecdotal evidence of other people's experiences in the witness box, or perhaps from dramatic representations of cross-examination, in which the starring, and usually glamorous, lawyer triumphantly demolishes the evidence of the key witness or produces material at the eleventh hour, as if out of a hat, which undermines the whole prosecution (or defence) case. These representations cannot give a realistic idea of the court process. Plays or films usually last less than three hours, which is little more than a morning in court. Any contested court hearing is likely to last at least one court day – five hours – and could be spread over several days. So, cross-examination is not usually a fast and furious encounter over ten or fifteen minutes, but can last an hour or more, or possibly even days.

For social workers facing cross-examination of their evidence, preparation and understanding the way in which advocates approach the task will help make the experience less daunting and more manageable. As the aim of cross-examination is to expose any flaws in the evidence, it follows that evidence which has been properly prepared and presented by people who are confident in their role, familiar with their material, clear about the rationale for any opinions expressed, and understand what is likely to happen, has the best chance of standing up to scrutiny. We have explored the importance of presentation and use of language and, as much as anything else, this will support you when facing cross-examination. However, it is also helpful to understand the purpose of cross-examination and how lawyers approach the task.

> ### RESEARCH SUMMARY
>
> *A recent study (Ellison and Wheatcroft, 2010) found that the witnesses who handled cross-examination best gave the fullest and most reliable answers. They were most likely to ask for questions to be clarified and were likely to have been given prior guidance on cross-examination techniques. Witnesses who received no preparation put more effort into dealing with cross-examination and tended to become nervous and frustrated as a result. The researchers suggest that lawyers' use of complex questions containing multiple parts, double-negatives and advanced vocabulary may affect the brain's ability to filter and streamline information, and that familiarisation 'frees up' capacity in the brain, enabling witnesses to organise their knowledge of events and improve their ability to respond to questions effectively.*

The purpose of cross-examination

Contrary to the impression often created by films and television, the purpose of cross-examination is not entertainment of the public through the discomfort of the witness, orchestrated by a seasoned verbal assassin, the barrister, like a form of modern gladiatorial combat. The only proper purpose of cross-examination is to give all parties in a case the opportunity, usually through their advocate, to challenge the evidence of other parties. In this way evidence can be tested for accuracy, consistency and authenticity. If a witness's evidence is accepted, there is no need for cross-examination, because there is nothing about which questions need to be asked. As it is only necessary to cross-examine witnesses on contested evidence, its scope may be quite narrow. If, however, a party wishes to challenge the way in which a local authority has managed the whole of a client's case, it may be necessary and appropriate for their advocate to ask the social worker numerous and detailed questions about what decisions were made, what actions were or were not taken, and why.

What are witnesses likely to be asked about in cross-examinations?

As we have seen, evidence comes in either or both of two categories – fact and opinion.

Evidence of fact is evidence of what a witness has perceived by use of their senses – that is, what they have seen, heard, touched, smelled or tasted.

Possible reasons for challenging evidence of fact include the following:

- **Perception** It may be suggested that a witness's perception at the time of the event in question was wrong; for example, that while observing a period of contact between a parent and child, something relevant happened which the witness did not notice, or which they did notice, but misunderstood or misinterpreted.

- **Memory** Evidence often relates to events which occurred months, or even years, previously and it could be suggested that a witness's memory has faded, so that relevant matters have been partially or completely forgotten, or inaccurately recalled. This is why timely, objective and comprehensive record-keeping is so important.

- **Bias or prejudice** Although not very likely in relation to professional witnesses, an advocate could suggest that a witness was biased or prejudiced against their client for some reason. Social workers usually have the benefit of professional supervision, which should ensure that facts are accurate, opinions are firmly based on evidence, and decisions are supported by a clear rationale. However, it is essential to maintain balance and objectivity, which may on occasions mean disclosing information which does not necessarily support the case of the party for whom you are giving evidence.

- **Lying** It is possible that a witness could be accused in cross-examination of deliberately giving an inaccurate account – telling lies. It is not expected that a social worker, or any professional witness, will ever tell lies on oath, and it is very unlikely that an advocate would consider it appropriate to suggest such a thing. Yet it is when that suggestion is made that cross-examination is most likely to become confrontational, distressing to the witness and more like how it is represented on television and in films. As we have seen, lawyers act under a set of professional rules and it is professional misconduct for a barrister to *make statements or ask questions which are merely scandalous or intended or calculated only to vilify, insult or annoy either a witness or some other person*. It follows that advocates should not make suggestions of lying or other discreditable conduct on the part of professional witnesses, unless it is necessary to their client's case to do so and there are solid grounds to support them.

Evidence of opinion is evidence of what the witness thinks about something. Usually, evidence of opinion may not be given in court. However, as we have seen, there is an exception in relation to matters requiring expert knowledge. Expert knowledge is acquired by training, experience, or a combination of both. If another party calls an expert witness who expresses a different opinion from the one you have formed, inevitably you will be cross-examined about it. On professional matters, different people legitimately can hold different views, which in itself is not a reason for criticism. However, in contested legal proceedings, where differences in professional opinion are important, one of the court's tasks is to decide which opinion to accept. Judges and magistrates are not equipped by academic or professional training to form opinions on professional social work issues, and so they must listen to those who express competing views and decide which to accept. They could accept neither and take a middle course, but their decisions must be based on relevant grounds of distinction between the different opinions.

Possible reasons for challenging evidence of opinion include the following:

- **Level of expertise** Structural engineers are qualified, and likely to be experienced, in the design of the structure of buildings. They are therefore, in law, experts, but only in relation to the design of the structure of buildings. They are not experts in child care, and no one would dream of suggesting that they were. To be qualified to give opinion evidence means being able to offer evidence which goes beyond a level of understanding which might be found in a person of reasonable intelligence and education. However, what is often found in family proceedings is overlapping evidence between different professionals. There may be medical, psychiatric or psychological evidence in addition to more than one source of social work evidence. A social worker's view about the best way to promote the future development of a child could differ from that of the child psychologist called on behalf of the parents. The children's guardian may not fully support the local authority's plan. In such cases the court has to decide which witness is best qualified to express an opinion on the matter in dispute. It cannot be said that the evidence of a psychologist or children's guardian should always be preferred to that of a social worker, or vice versa, since everything depends on the issues in the case. However, where there is disputed evidence, cross-examination of the social worker will have as one of its objectives to demonstrate to the court that the social worker is not as well-equipped as the other professionals to express an opinion. This type of cross-examination should not be a cause of distress, since it is not a criticism of someone with one set of professional qualifications that they do not possess a different set of professional qualifications. This is so, even if the court ultimately decides that one person is better qualified to express a view than another. Each of us claims some knowledge of the law relating to social work, and where the issue was essentially legal, such as the interpretation of an Act of Parliament, you may prefer the opinion of the legally qualified author. If, however, the issue was essentially one of social work practice, you would be likely to consider the opinion of the qualified social worker as more valuable. So it is with differing opinion evidence from professionals from different disciplines. However, we acknowledge that it can be frustrating when other expert witnesses appear to overstep what you consider are professional boundaries when expressing their opinions. In such cases it is important to avoid being defensive, and to remain focused on the rationale for the opinions you have formed.

- **Level of experience** We do not want to overemphasise the significance of this, but if two social workers who express different opinions are, on the one hand, someone newly qualified and inexperienced and, on the other, a highly qualified person with many years' practice experience, the court may prefer the evidence of the latter. In such a case, the cross-examination of the newly qualified social worker might have as one of its aims to demonstrate that they lacked sufficient experience. This should not be taken as personal criticism, since no one can produce experience which they do not have.

- **Range of experience** Although social work qualifying training is generic, most social work practice and post-qualifying training is specialist, and a social worker will usually only be working with one specific client group at any one time. Consequently, a social worker with many years' experience of mental health work, who has recently moved into a child care post, could have it suggested in cross-examination that their limited experience of child care casts doubt on the validity of their opinions in a family case. Again, this should not be taken as a personal criticism, and we suggest that if you are a qualified social worker you should feel confident in the value of your generic training, supported by registration requirements in relation to continuing professional development.

- **Rationale** Notwithstanding what we have said about qualifications and experience, it is far from inevitable that the court will prefer the evidence of the more experienced practitioner if the newly qualified social worker has valid grounds for their opinions, which are clearly and confidently expressed. It is therefore essential that, when preparing for cross-examination, you should have a good grasp of the rationale behind the opinions you have put forward, incorporating the four Rs described in Chapter 7. In complex cases, there may be differences of view within your agency as to what should constitute the plan recommended to the court. If this happens you need to debate and, if necessary, challenge these differences before the final hearing. If they persist, you must inform the legal team representing your agency, since any lack of commitment or confidence on your part is likely to become apparent during cross-examination.

How advocates approach cross-examination

Advocacy, which includes conducting cross-examination, is part of legal training, and the College of Law introduces law students to the skills of cross-examination in this way:

> *In order to conduct cross-examination effectively, it is necessary to develop a 'theory' of the client's case. This theory should be a plausible version of the events, consistent with the available evidence and the client's instructions which, if accepted, will result in the court finding in the client's favour.*

> (Elkington et al., 2010, page 162)

Some lawyers believe that skills in cross-examination cannot be taught but depend more on learning by experience. Surprisingly, a number of eminent barristers have not been very effective cross-examiners and others do not particularly enjoy the process. However, for many, cross-examination represents the point at which their legal knowledge and advocacy skills come together in an exercise which is potentially challenging, exciting or even exhilarating. We recall the long-awaited opportunity to cross-examine a particularly notorious witness in a long-running case as one of the highlights of a legal career.

An effective cross-examiner is one who succeeds in obtaining from another party's witness evidence which assists their client's case, which means obtaining answers which the witness accepts are accurate, or at least more accurate than their previous evidence. After cross-examination, the advocate for the party calling a witness can ask further questions to clarify answers given in cross-examination. This stage of the evidence is called re-examination and is limited to any issues which have arisen out of cross-examination, rather than going over evidence which has already been given. If a witness has been persuaded by the style of cross-examination to say something which they did not mean, this is likely to become apparent in re-examination when there is an opportunity to correct the previous answer. The cross-examiner is therefore looking to achieve an impact which cannot be reversed in re-examination, which depends on presenting the witness with material which changes their perception of the fact or opinion about which they are being asked. Clearly, anxiety or confusion can influence a witness's responses, which is why we hope that understanding of the process will make this less likely to occur.

Effective cross-examination depends upon thorough preparation and good command of the material available. It is worth remembering that if an advocate puts a question during cross-examination which suggests that there exists a relevant document to support the point of the question, this is probably true, because it will have been found during the preparation of the case. It would be unwise for a cross-examiner to suggest to a witness a version of events which could not be supported by reference to evidence. It used to be said that student barristers were told: *Never ask a question to which you do not know the answer*. That may be apocryphal, but it does illustrate that in order to try to persuade a witness to agree to, or change their mind about, something, the cross-examiner needs to be in command of all the relevant facts and able to produce supporting material.

The most basic style of cross-examination, and that most familiar from films and television, is somewhat as follows:

Cross-examiner: I put it to you that your evidence is a pack of lies.

Witness: No, it isn't.

Cross-examiner: Yes, it is.

Witness: No, it isn't.

This is more reminiscent of a pantomime than the courtroom. Only once in a professional career did one of us suggest to a witness that his participation in a particular enterprise was a means of stealing money and, surprisingly, receive the answer *yes*. Barring the odd exception, cross-examination by putting an accusation to a witness, and repeating it if they do not agree, is a waste of time, although it does happen. Effective cross-examination depends upon producing material which persuades a witness to alter their evidence and, if such material exists, in the majority of cases it is in documentary form.

Styles of cross-examination

Having said that cross-examination is a rather inexact science, there are nevertheless discernible styles which can be observed, sometimes in combination.

- **Organised and predictable** Some quite eminent and successful lawyers prepare thoroughly for cross-examination to the extent of writing out a list of questions in advance. Cross-examination then takes the form of going through the questions. This is not especially difficult to handle, because the questions are usually posed in the order in which they have been written, without regard to any answers given in the meantime.

- **Intellectually challenging** Cross-examiners who maintain the intellectual flexibility to pursue answers which seem relevant to their client's case will have an outline plan which they adjust as required. Many advocates are able to think on their feet, adapting their questions according to the material obtained in the course of the cross-examination. They may also try to unsettle the witness by taking events out of chronological order or by suddenly changing the subject. This kind of cross-examination can be very tiring for witnesses.

- **Intimidating** Occasionally advocates set out to dominate and intimidate witnesses with a loud, hectoring voice and patronising manner. This may have some theatrical appeal, but is usually less effective than a quieter, more respectful style. If a witness's answers in cross-examination have been obtained by an advocate who has been sympathetic and courteous, they may well appear more persuasive to the court. This is particularly true in family proceedings, where advocates are expected to avoid an adversarial approach and the primary focus is the welfare of the child, rather than who wins or loses.

- **Chaotic** While not exactly a style of cross-examination, you may be surprised to find that some advocates seem incapable of asking a simple question and pose several questions at once, often incorporating statements, while expecting one *yes* or *no* answer. This is not usually a deliberate ploy to confuse the witness, but rather evidence of the limitations of the advocate as a cross-examiner.

- **Unprepared** A variation on the chaotic is the cross-examiner who is simply not on top of the material and whose questions are based on a misunderstanding, or lack of knowledge, of the facts or issues in the case. Unfortunately, this seems to be becoming more common as restrictions on public funding of legal costs influence the time which advocates have for, or are prepared to devote to, preparing for cross-examination. While many advocates are competent at cross-examination and are conscientious in its preparation, you should not assume that all lawyers are skilled cross-examiners.

- **Softening-up** Some advocates adopt a technique which involves asking a series of fairly innocuous, simple and uncontroversial questions before moving on to a more assertive line of questioning. The hope is that the witness will relax and continue to agree when more contentious matters are put to them.

- **Unpleasant or nasty** There are, regrettably, a few advocates whose manner is bullying, sarcastic and intended to cause confusion and discomfort to witnesses while remaining, by a whisker, within their rules of professional conduct. Sometimes this approach incorporates shock tactics intended to distract a witness from the focus of their evidence as, for example, in opening cross-examination with a question such as *Do you always find it difficult to tell the truth?* Fortunately this style of cross-examination is not often encountered, particularly in family proceedings, but if you do experience it, be assured that it is not a legitimate technique, but rather a reflection of the personality, and possibly professional inadequacy, of the advocate. Such behaviour will not pass the judge unnoticed, and may well be the subject of judicial censure.

Types of question

In social work interviews a distinction is made between open and closed questions and these are also used to different effect in cross-examination. For example, a closed question may be used to press for an admission of some sort when a witness would prefer to add explanatory material, or qualify their answer, while an open question may be put to test a witness's understanding of a complex issue. However, closed or leading questions tend to be preferred in cross-examination as the advocate potentially retains more control over the process.

There are three broad categories of cross-examination question – probing, insinuating and confrontational – each of which may trigger a different emotional response. As an expert witness, you are most likely to encounter the first type, which are easiest to deal with if you follow the advice below about listening carefully to the question, keeping your answer brief and focused, and avoiding jargon and clichés. Insinuating and confrontational questions are more difficult, since your first reaction may be defensiveness, or even irritation. Although in principle you are not allowed to ask questions yourself, it may be worth asking what the actual question is in these circumstances. The following example, in which the advocate seems to be suggesting that because it was an unusual case it should not have received a routine response, shows that it is sometimes possible to deflect an insinuation, gain some extra thinking time and reduce it to something more manageable. It also illustrates an advocate twice failing to formulate a proper question.

CASE STUDY **10.1**

Victoria Climbié Inquiry, 4 October 2001

Q: But this case was not quite the ordinary case that you were dealing with, simply housing issues, because you have noted some of your other concerns about the case; the fact that she has children in France and intends to return.

A: Was that a question?

Q: Yes.

A: What was the question?

Q: Well, it seems looking at it that there are issues that go beyond the simple case of housing ... it was not quite the average case you were dealing with.

A: Well, it was not an average case because she did come from France and part of her family was in France.

Confrontational questions sometimes follow probing questions if the cross-examiner considers it worth pressing for particular answers. This is another reason why focused responses are important. Vagueness or elusiveness in an answer may encourage the advocate to become more confrontational in an effort to extract some kind of admission.

The construction of questions can sometimes prove problematic for witnesses, particularly anxious ones. Lawyers are not known for the simplicity of their language and practices such as the use of double negatives or the inclusion of several subclauses can make it difficult for witnesses to understand the crux of the question. Again, rather than risk giving a misleading answer, we encourage you to ask for clarification if it is not clear what you are being asked.

Unlike in examination in chief, advocates can ask leading questions during cross-examination and often such questions are presented as statements upon which the witness is in effect invited to comment.

How to handle cross-examination

1. Know the case inside out – don't rely on reports from others.

2. Don't leave all your thinking until you get to court.

3. Read and reread all the evidence and reports submitted to court until you know most of it by heart.

4. Anticipate what the other parties are likely to disagree with.

5. Ask your supervisor to play 'devil's advocate' to help test your evidence.

6. Keep your diary clear for the day before the hearing.

7. Above all, consider how you can be of most assistance to the court.   (Child care team manager)

Figure 10.1 Advice for preparing for cross-examination

While too much preparation can be counterproductive in that it can fuel anxiety and deflect you from the main issues in the case, it is worth identifying strategies which may support you in the witness box.

- **Don't take it personally** Always try to approach cross-examination in a professional manner, which, as you will know from your practice, requires resilience, assertiveness and detachment. In asking questions, advocates are performing their professional duty to their client, which may mean that they are asked to put to you something that you regard as outrageous (for example, that you have been racist in your dealings with someone). If this happens, try not to take personally any suggestions made, even if you feel that they reflect on your professional competence. In any event, your professional competence is not, as already explained, something to feel oversensitive about, even if another party's expert may appear to be better qualified, to have more experience or simply hold another view. It is important to appear calm, objective and in control, both verbally and non-verbally. Even though you may feel indignant, or even insulted, nothing is gained by showing this, and it may harm your credibility as a professional witness if you reveal your personal feelings.

PRACTITIONER REFLECTION **10.1**

I remember fighting a losing battle with the tendency to place my hands on my hips during a very long and drawn-out cross-examination, thus unfortunately suggesting an attitude which was more confrontational than conciliatory. This would have been less of a problem had I been sitting down.

(A social worker)

- **Are you going to play the game?** Although cross-examining advocates have the advantage of knowing the rules of evidence, and are able to determine the question agenda, they do not hold all the cards. To a skilled advocate, cross-examination is essentially an intellectual game for two players, one of whom is you. Most importantly from your point of view, the advocate cannot play without you, which critical fact gives you more control over the process than you may imagine. For example, if you are unable, or do not wish, to give the answer for which the advocate hopes, no one can force you to do so.

- **Establish the ground rules** As we have seen, if a question is confusing, you are entitled to say that you do not understand it and ask for it to be clarified. If you think that a document may help you answer, you are entitled to ask to be shown it. You are not normally permitted to ask questions of the person questioning you, unless it is for clarification. However, the advocate cannot fix the ground rules as to how you answer the questions. Sometimes an advocate will try to insist that a witness answers a question with *yes* or *no,* when neither would be a sufficient answer. Just say that the question cannot be answered with a simple *yes* or *no,* and give the answer that you want to give. The court is interested in knowing what your evidence is, not what the advocate wishes it to be. Remember, too, that you are there to assist the court, not the advocates.

- **Expect the unexpected** You cannot assume that you will be asked about events in chronological order. This is likely to be the order in which they are dealt with in your witness statement, but as we have seen, one approach to cross-examination is to take events out of order, so as to unsettle the witness, expose any flaws in their overall grasp of the facts or issues in the case, and perhaps persuade them to change their view. Other techniques include taking the witness by surprise by changing the subject, or asking essentially the same question in a different form, hoping to demonstrate inconsistency if the answers vary. These possibilities make it all the more important to listen carefully to the questions and to give considered answers. If you think a question you have already answered is being repeated, take control by saying something like 'I believe I've already answered that question. Can I be of any further assistance to the court?'

- **Think outside of the box** When you find yourself in a stressful or challenging situation as in court, it is easy, but dangerous, to adapt your thinking or make assumptions to fit the overall view you have formed of the case. Without good supervision you may be unaware of this tendency, but it is important always to keep in mind that the court, in seeking to reach a good decision, will want to explore every possibility and ensure that the evidence to support a particular plan stands up to scrutiny. Therefore, you should be prepared to be questioned about the extent to which you considered alternative options or courses of action other than the ones that were adopted or are recommended, and to describe any preparatory, therapeutic or experimental work you have done in that context. This is particularly likely to happen if there is disagreement between the experts in the case.

- **Control the pace** It is possible to gain thinking time by carefully considering each question and taking time to formulate your answer. The judge is likely to intervene if questions are fired so fast as to give a witness insufficient time to answer, but if you need time to consider your answer you should ask for it. Exerting control in this way will also help redress any perceived power imbalance between you and the advocate.

The court was considering the issue of permanency in relation to two boys. They had been found to be difficult to manage together in foster care and the local authority, supported by an independent expert, recommended that separate adoption placements would offer the best opportunity to address each boy's differing and complex needs. The children's guardian thought that there was a strong attachment between the boys and that they should remain together. In cross-examination at the final hearing the social worker was questioned on behalf of the children's guardian about why the local authority proposal to separate the boys had not been tested by means of a bridging placement or temporary care for one or other of the boys, what the plan was for future contact between them, and the nature of the evidence which existed to support such a plan. Although the local authority had not wished to appear to be pre-empting the court's decision, the social worker's inability to satisfy the court that this preparatory work had been done undermined the local authority's proposals, resulting in an adjournment and consequent delay in progressing arrangements to settle the boys' future care.

- **Expect to be fairly treated** One of the judge's responsibilities is to ensure that witnesses are treated fairly. The example below illustrates the fact that advocates are sometimes tempted to make comments during cross-examination. This should not happen, and although the judge or your own advocate ought to be alert to any improper comments made, unfortunately they do not always achieve the necessary level of alertness. While you should not be oversensitive, if you feel that an advocate is being unfair or even offensive, you can appeal to the judge, who will decide whether it is necessary to intervene. However, an advocate may feel that it is worth risking the censure of the judge in order to attach a potentially negative connotation to a particular witness.

During cross-examination, I was asked to explain the description 'manipulative' which I had unwisely included in a case record some time previously (when I was, of course, very inexperienced!). The cross-examining advocate commented: 'It seems to me that social workers apply this description to anyone who dares to disagree with them', at which point the judge intervened, saying to the advocate, Miss S, 'That is an offensive remark and you will withdraw it'. However, the advocate was doubtless satisfied by the fact that the comment had been heard. Needless to say, I have never used the word 'manipulative' since.

(A social worker)

- **Don't try to second guess** It is usually a mistake to anticipate where the line of questioning is going since you may be tempted to prepare what you consider to be the *correct* answer, rather than giving the answer that you actually believe to be the truth. You may also come across to the court as someone who is not being completely open and honest.

- **Watch out for the wolf in sheep's clothing** Beware of agreeing too readily with apparently innocuous propositions, especially if they do not relate to you personally.

As we have seen, sometimes advocates will try to soften up witnesses with apparently straightforward and uncontroversial questions before pressing more strongly for more contentious admissions. You should also take care before agreeing with statements put to you as questions in cross-examination, since the words chosen by the advocate may be subtly, but possibly significantly, different from those you would have chosen.

- **Keep it short** It is usually best to give as brief an answer as possible. This is most help-ful to the judge, who has to concentrate on the central issues in the case and make a note of the oral evidence, and is also likely to be beneficial to you. Long or unfocused answers provide the opportunity for points to be made which might not otherwise have been obvious to the cross-examiner. In a case about a harbour in which one of us was involved, a witness described himself as a port expert. At the start of his cross-examination he was routinely asked, 'You describe yourself as a port expert?' Instead of simply agreeing, he delivered a long account of why he had so described himself, which revealed that his expertise was limited to the operation of one particular port and, con-sequently, he was not entitled to be regarded as an expert in ports generally.

- **Keep it simple** As in written records and reports, when responding to oral questions you should avoid using jargon, acronyms, clichés or expressions which might not readily be understood by any of the parties.

- **Focus, focus, focus** You should confine your answer to the scope of the question posed and not introduce new material unless absolutely necessary, otherwise there is a risk that you will alert the cross-examiner to a line of questioning not previously considered relevant. The following case study shows a cross-examiner being offered an unexpected admission by a witness who had not carefully considered the question posed.

CASE STUDY **10.3**

Victoria Climbié Inquiry, 4 October 2001

Q: Here we are at the beginning of June and you were still being asked to do an assess-ment. Did that surprise you, or is that normal?

A: I think at the time it was difficult. We usually assessed people via housing needs, rather than being child-focused.

Q: You assessed people generally on housing needs rather than being child-focused?

A: Yes, at the time.

- **Maintain objectivity** As in all aspects of court work you must continue to demonstrate fairness and balance during cross-examination, notwithstanding the possibility that you may feel under pressure or even, at times, under attack. This means giving credit where it is due and ensuring that you do not overlook, or minimise the significance of, rel-evant matters which may not necessarily support the professional opinions presented in your evidence. For example, if you were questioned about your assessment that a parent lacks commitment based on their unreliability in the context of contact arrange-ments, you should also mention when they arrived on time, even if it was only once or twice. While you should never duck your duty accurately to describe facts and offer your honest opinion, you should also consider the impact of the words you choose when conveying information with a potentially negative connotation.

ACTIVITY 10.1

In relation to the following examples taken from social work evidence, identify alternative ways of expressing the information verbally which do not detract from the central message, but which are less judgemental in tone.

- *I found out that he had been lying again about his whereabouts, although he persisted in denying it.*
- *After giving the relationship several more chances, she eventually told him she had had enough and fled to her sister's house.*
- *She was very unco-operative and extremely aggressive and hostile towards me, both verbally and non-verbally.*
- *There were two open cans of lager on the table and while I was there he opened a third.*
- *The house smelt of cigarettes and dogs and the children's bedroom was poorly furnished and in chaos.*

- **Admit mistakes** It is very unlikely that everything you do in practice will stand up to detailed scrutiny, especially with the benefit of hindsight. If possible, you should explore with your advocate in advance of the hearing any potential areas of difficulty which might become the focus of cross-examination, so that you are both prepared for the issue to be raised. If it is suggested that something should have been done differently, be as honest as you can and admit any shortfall in your practice. Nothing is gained by trying to defend the indefensible or making excuses for errors or omissions, and by acknowledging a mistake you are demonstrating that you are aware of the requirements of good social work practice. Nevertheless, try not to let any admissions of this nature detract from the central issues in the case. In the case study below, we suggest that the social worker could usefully have included the words we have added, not in italics.

CASE STUDY 10.4

Victoria Climbié Inquiry, 4 October 2001

Q: Do you accept that file entry is not signed or dated?

A: I think my name appears at the bottom.

Q: Yes, sorry, but not dated?

A: No, it is not dated.

Q: Do you accept that is a shortfall?

A: **Absolutely, yes,** *but it should not detract from the matters contained within that file entry.*

If you say something during cross-examination which you later realise is not right, or which you think may have been misleading, it is important to say so. If you leave it, hoping that no one has noticed, you risk being accused of inconsistency or inaccuracy if the matter is raised subsequently. Simply saying, 'I think I might have given the wrong impression when I said …' or 'I realise I made a mistake in my last reply …' should guard against this, although avoid making too effusive an apology as it might suggest that you lack professional confidence. You must also take care if suggesting that an external factor was to blame for any shortfall to which you admit, since you are likely to be asked what you did about it. If you did nothing, and this is the first time that you have mentioned it, then it is probably unwise to refer to it.

CASE STUDY **10.5**

Victoria Climbié Inquiry, 4 October 2001

Q: Was the supervision you received from your team manager adequate?

A: Not at that time, no it was not.

Q: Did you do anything to refer your concerns about this to senior managers?

- **You can't duck questions** When giving evidence, or being cross-examined, you cannot normally refuse to answer a question. There is an exception in most court proceedings if, by giving a truthful answer, you might lay yourself open to possible criminal charges. However, this does not apply to cases involving children (s.98 Children Act 1989) because the welfare of children is paramount and therefore overrides all other considerations.

- **Use notes with care** As with giving evidence, you can refer to notes during cross-examination, but there is a potential pitfall. If you use notes to refresh your memory, lawyers for the other parties in the case will ask to look at them. Social work records are usually contained in the case file which you will have to hand over, giving everyone the opportunity to look at the whole file. As it is usually unrealistic to rely on memory when being cross-examined, it is important to anticipate this by writing your records in such a way as to make your files fit to be shown to other people who may have different interests in the case. You will also normally be asked how long after the event you made your records, and if you cannot confirm that they were made contemporaneously, or at least within a day or so, their accuracy may be placed in doubt.

- **Maintain formality** Court proceedings are essentially formal and serious occasions and it is important to remember how much is likely to be at stake for one or more of the parties. Some relaxation may occur during the course of a hearing, particularly a lengthy one in which the participants become more familiar with the process and each other, but witnesses should not take the initiative in this respect and attempts at humour can go spectacularly wrong. One of us was once involved in a case in which an issue was whether the witness had been present when HM Queen Elizabeth had officially opened a building. He was asked in cross-examination how the Queen had arrived at the opening ceremony and replied, 'On a bicycle'. Not surprisingly, his evidence on that, but also on other more important matters, was subsequently rejected.

PRACTITIONER REFLECTION **10.3**

The best social workers answer questions in cross-examination fairly and honourably, concede a little if necessary but, as is their duty, stick to their guns. For example: 'Yes, I agree that David is much better at controlling his temper and the school is pleased. However, I think we still have a long way to go. The parents love him very much and he loves them, but I still don't think that they can give him the care he needs.'

(A family court judge)

The practical application of this advice is illustrated by means of extracts from two recent family court judgements, which included an assessment of social workers' cross-examination evidence:

> *Under cross-examination the social worker accepted that the mother has a good attachment to the children although B still displays some difficult behaviour at times. B's speech has improved since going into foster care but there are still concerns and he has been seen by a speech and language therapist. He is seen to benefit from one to one attention whilst at nursery. The social worker accepted that this could make B more difficult to place with an adoptive family, but not significantly so, and he is making progress all the time. I accept the evidence of the social worker.*

(Re B and A (Children) [2010] EWMC 11 (FPC))

> *Cross-examination of the social worker revealed that the decision of the local authority to plan for long-term adoption was made at an early stage based on earlier assessments from previous proceedings. Further, it was revealed that the social worker did not discuss the final care plan with the parents. The contents were conveyed through solicitors. Her reason for this was that she was told that the parents had made a complaint about her. We consider that the parents could have been treated more sympathetically.*

(X Council v Mother & Ors [2010] EWMC 7 (FPC))

ACTIVITY **10.2**

Although you should never coach anyone on their evidence, it is possible to practise techniques for dealing with cross-examination.

- *Share something you have written with a colleague or friend and ask them to discover more about its content and your opinion of it by asking you a variety of types of question (open, closed, probing, insinuating, challenging, confrontational).*

- *If possible, have an observer assess the effectiveness of different types of question and the nature of the responses obtained. Reflect on the process and your reactions with your questioner and observer and swap roles.*

After cross-examination

After cross-examination the lawyer on whose behalf the witness was called has the opportunity to re-examine them to clarify any outstanding points. Don't try to leave the witness box as soon as cross-examination is over, although it is tempting. However, re-examination does not happen in every case. Whether or not there is re-examination, it is conventional for the lawyer who has called a witness to ask if there is anything the judge wishes to ask. Judges differ as to how they obtain information from witnesses. Some leave it all to the lawyers and ask few, if any, questions. This does not mean that the judge has not been interested in your evidence, but rather that everything necessary has been covered. Some judges ask questions during the cross-examination or re-examination as matters occur to them, and others save up everything to the end. If a judge asks questions at the end of the evidence or cross-examination, the lawyers usually are given the opportunity to ask any further questions which arise out of those questions and the witness's responses.

Davis, L (2007) *See you in court: a social worker's guide to presenting evidence in care proceedings.* London: Jessica Kingsley.

This text includes an appendix with transcripts of short cross-examination exchanges involving social workers, illustrating different techniques employed by advocates.

www.nationalarchives.gov.uk/ERORecords/VC/2/2/Evidence/Archive/

The extensive transcripts of the public inquiry into events surrounding the death of Victoria Climbié provide a fascinating insight into the reality of cross-examination.

www.scie.org.uk/publications/elearning/law/law05/index.asp

The Social Care Institute for Excellence offers e-learning materials to support the development of court skills, including facing cross-examination.

Chapter 11
What happens next?

This chapter will help you to meet the following National Occupational Standard for social work.

- Key role 2: Plan, carry out, review and evaluate social work practice with individuals, families, carers, groups and communities, and other professionals.
  - Review the outcomes with individuals, families, carers, groups, communities, organisations, professionals and others.

Introduction

After a case is over, the lawyers are likely to move on to the next one without much of a backward glance. Although courts usually seek to minimise any negative consequences of their decisions, they are accustomed to the fact that most of them will result in at least one dissatisfied or aggrieved party. However, social workers and service users are likely to have to work with the consequences for a considerable time afterwards.

Social workers often describe their court experiences as the most demanding of their career. Sometimes they are viewed negatively, but with effective preparation and support court work offers opportunities and challenges which do not arise in other areas of work. After it is over, we encourage you to reflect on what happened to help you both personally and professionally, not just to survive, but to develop and thrive. We also urge you to ensure that service users' needs remain central to your practice.

First reactions

For professionals, initial, instinctive reactions must be followed by a more reflective response. This is important to support work needed to re-establish effective relationships with service users, colleagues and other professionals, and for your own well-being and development. If this does not happen, there is a risk of overly defensive practice, in which social workers take action to avoid being criticised for not taking action (SCIE, 2005, page 173).

Reflection

The action of the mind by which it is conscious of its own operations; contemplation; to consider meditatively, with the implication of censure.

(Chambers dictionary)

Identified by Schön (1983) as an important constituent of professional learning, reflection is an essential prerequisite for the cultivation of self-awareness and your future professional development. Relief leads to relaxation and it is tempting to avoid further professional demands after a challenging court experience. However, it is essential to make time for critical reflection, preferably supported by effective supervision.

- Pay attention to fleeting thoughts, particularly out of context.
- Seek connections between things which you usually consider separately.
- Seek contrasting aspects within a situation which you usually see as integrated.
- Place single events within a wider context.
- Think about the direction in which current circumstances or assumptions could change.
- Think experimentally – 'What if ...?'
- Reframe questions.
- Mentally place yourself in the shoes of others.
- Analyse your thinking, preferably with the help of good supervision.

Figure 11.1 Some ideas to encourage reflection

ACTIVITY **11.1**

After any court experience, reflect on how it went.

- *How would you describe your overall experience?*
- *What aspects of your preparation were most useful?*
- *What were you pleased about?*
- *What did you find difficult?*
- *What did you not understand?*
- *What most surprised you?*
- *What do you wish you had done differently?*
- *What do you wish you had known about in advance?*
- *What did you think about the behaviour and performance of others?*
- *What have you learned which will help you in the future?*
- *How will you use this to support and prepare others?*

Developing internal checklists in this way will ensure that every experience can be used productively, both for your own and for others' benefit.

The needs of service users

Afterwards, if your service users are angry or upset, ensure that you or someone else makes contact within a few days. It may be difficult, but doing nothing will almost certainly be more harmful.

(CAFCASS manager)

After a challenging experience it is difficult to take time to consider the feelings of others in addition to your own, but as a professional, this is what you must do. The needs and reactions of people who have been personally, as opposed to professionally, involved in court proceedings are individual and unpredictable (Williams, 1999, page 51), and while there may be some identifiable patterns, it is wrong to make generalisations. Depending on the type of case, possible responses range from fear, disbelief, shame, anger, guilt, resentment, humiliation or grief, to those of relief or a determination to make positive life changes.

At one level the justice system can be understood as the major institutional way we deal with losses, largely around our expectations of how other people will behave towards us. These losses range from minor slights, where our sense of fairness is challenged, to more serious encounters where our homes are invaded, to severe assaults.

(Dawes in Thompson, ed, 2002, page 174)

Any court experience is likely to involve loss for one or more of the people involved. Potential losses range from those which are severe and permanent, such as a decision to place a child for adoption, to those from which recovery is possible and lessons can be learned, such as the restriction of liberty by means of a community sentence or having a part of your evidence rejected by a court.

ACTIVITY *11.2*

Identify the different types of loss which might be experienced by people after legal proceedings, both civil and criminal, distinguishing between losses which are permanent, those which are likely to be temporary and those about which it cannot be predicted whether they will be permanent or temporary.

It is not within the scope of this book to explore different models and theories of loss, analyse the variety of cultural needs arising in people experiencing loss, or explore in detail the range of possible professional responses. However, the knowledge base of social work will help you anticipate possible reactions, which clearly can have implications for working with service users in the aftermath of court proceedings. Extreme reactions to loss are most likely from people who have limited personal resources, those who have unacknowledged, unresolved or interrupted previous experience of loss, and those who are already under stress, all likely to apply to many situations in which you are involved professionally. Reactions can include the following, either singly or, more usually, in combination:

- Refusal to accept what has happened, or a feeling of disconnection with reality, sometimes described as *watching oneself on a stage*.

- Resentment and blame.

- Withdrawal from painful reminders.

- Resurfacing of previous experiences of loss.

- Feelings of vulnerability, with impaired ability to cope with minor events.

- Physical symptoms, such as poor appetite or changed sleep patterns.

- Loss of interest in or ability to maintain social contacts, or even a wish to move away.

- Guilt.

- Anger.

- Low mood or depression.

These reactions may be observed months, or even years, after the event and an ability to anticipate them is important. For example, a mother who refuses to take part in a planning meeting following a court hearing may be unable to cope at that time with the feelings that it arouses. This does not necessarily mean that she does not ever want to be involved with her child's future, and her raw emotions are more likely to heal if they are accepted, rather than resisted, challenged or ignored. Although initially you may not be in a position to mitigate service users' reactions to any great extent, pain is likely to be exacerbated by lack of thought, empathy or foresight. This is illustrated by the next case study, which shows how the needs of service users can be overlooked and demonstrates the importance of continuing sensitivity and commitment on your part.

CASE STUDY 11.1

A local authority had initiated care proceedings in relation to a six-year-old boy, and his mother accepted the advice she was given that it was likely that a care order would be made and an adoption placement sought. However, she courageously gave evidence in court to demonstrate that although she could not look after her son, she cared about what happened to him. Although the judge was kind to her, she found the experience almost overwhelming and afterwards was extremely distressed. With the support of her solicitor, she wrote a letter to her son, which did not dispute the decision, but which told him how much she loved him and wanted him to have a happy life. The letter was handed to the social worker but when later the mother asked if her son had received the letter she was told it had been lost.

Although there is not sufficient background information here to enable us to offer a view on how the letter should have been dealt with in the interests of the child, we do suggest that a grieving mother's heartfelt expression of feelings deserved more respect. If, due to the circumstances of any particular case, you do not feel that any support from you is likely to be effective, at least in the short term, then you should consider possible alternatives, rather than leave people to cope alone.

In family cases remember, too, that although most of your dealings at court will have been with parents or those with parental responsibility, the needs and feelings of the children involved are unlikely to coincide with those of the adults, and merit special care and attention.

RESEARCH SUMMARY

Research undertaken into parents' perceptions of professional practice in public law child care and adoption proceedings (Smeeton and Boxall, 2010) found evidence of deep distress and sense of abandonment:

> *'She [the social worker] said they'd been adopted and you can't see them and they hadn't been adopted and I could see them, but they wouldn't let me anywhere near them.'*

> *'It was awful. I didn't want to turn up because I knew it would hurt me and I had to turn up just to say goodbye. It was really hard, I didn't want to leave them.'*

> *'I got no support when the kids were taken off me. I got no support when they went up for adoption. I got no support from anywhere at all.'*

Research carried out into the experiences of children who had been the subject of family court proceedings found that many young people felt that what happened after court was not always what they had been led to expect: 'Social workers say they want you to get on with a normal life, but it never really happens' (Ofsted, 2010b, page 16). They thought that social workers could offer better support to children who are unlikely to return to their families as a result of a court decision.

FURTHER READING

Currer, C (2007) *Loss and social work.* Exeter: Learning Matters.

Explores theoretical models of grieving, loss and change, and their practical application.

Williams, B (1999) *Working with victims of crime.* London: Jessica Kingsley.

Examines the needs and responses of victims to particular types of crime.

Conclusion

The central theme of this book is that of building bridges between the law and social work, in the interests of both social workers and service users. To achieve this, we have explained legal processes as they relate to courts, explored some of the dilemmas and challenges which you may face when undertaking court work, and offered ideas and suggestions on how to develop your courtroom and recording skills.

Preston-Shoot (2000) suggests that to demonstrate competence in legal settings social workers must be:

- Confident – to challenge.

- Credible – in presenting the rationale for decision-making.

- Critical – to make their practice and legal rules accessible to those with whom they work, to assess the impact of policies on people's lives and to navigate through questions of ethics, rights and needs.

- Creative – in order to exploit the possibilities that legal rules present, and to manage the practice dilemmas and conflicting imperatives that the interface between law and social work practice generates.

In encouraging you to develop these skills, we support the premise that what is needed is a *kind of new professional, who understands that middle ground, where law meets social work, and can bring together the principles and values they have in common* (SCIE, 2005, page 171). We accept that court proceedings can appear to be something of a game; this is not to deny their seriousness for those involved, but we suggest that many professional decision-making settings are similar in this respect. Case conferences, reviews, adoption and funding panels, planning, partnership and family group conference meetings all involve rules and tactics, the understanding of which is essential in order to take a full part and achieve good-quality decisions.

We have shown that the legal profession shares some key ethical principles with social work, and that remaining true to the values of your profession will maximise the effectiveness of your role. We encourage you to aspire to the highest possible standards of both spoken and written communication, and to regard court work as a unique opportunity, where the robustness of your practice and knowing the rules can make a key difference to the experience of service users (SCIE, 2005, page 174). We hope that we have been able to equip you with some useful resources and because the law, like social work, is subject to constant change, these will provide you with a framework for your continuing professional development.

> *Where law meets social work, there may be a new mix of skills that brings together the principles and values of both professions and applies them to the task of developing lawful, ethical social work practice. Service users are keen to witness such a development, and for social workers and lawyers to see themselves as allies in the task of promoting rights and justice.*

(SCIE, 2005, page 187)

References

Ames, N (1999) Social work recording: A new look at an old issue. *Journal of Social Work Education,* 35(2): 227–37.

Argyle, M (1994) *The psychology of interpersonal behaviour* (5th edition). London: Penguin Books.

Aston, J, Hill, D and Tackey, N (2006) *The Experience of Claimants in Race Discrimination Employment Tribunal Cases.* Employment Relations Research Series ERS55. London: Department of Trade and Industry.

Baker, J H (2002) *An Introduction to English Legal History* (4th edition). London: Butterworths.

Bar Council (2004) *Code of Conduct of the Bar of England and Wales* (8th edition). London: The Bar Council.

Bar Council (2005) *Guidance on Witness Preparation.* London: The Bar Council.

Bar Standards Board (2009) *Complaints and Hearings Performance Report.* London: BSB.

Bateman, N (2000) *Advocacy Skills for Health and Social Care Professionals* (2nd edition). London: Jessica Kingsley.

Beckett, C and Maynard, A (2005) *Values and Ethics in Social Work.* London: Sage.

Beckett, C, McKeigue, B and Taylor, H (2007) Coming to conclusions: social workers' perceptions of the decision-making process in care proceedings. *Child and Family Social Work,* 12(1): 54–63.

Beckett, C and McKeigue, B (2010) Objects of concern: caring for children during care proceedings. *British Journal of Social Work,* 40(7): 2086–2101.

Bond, C, Solon, M, Harper, P and Davies, G (2007) *The Expert Witness: a practical guide* (3rd edition). Crayford: Shaw & Sons.

Bond, T and Sandhu, A (2005) *Therapists in Court: providing evidence and supporting witnesses.* London: Sage.

Booth, T and Booth, W (2004) *Parents with learning difficulties, child protection and the courts*. Report to the Nuffield Foundation.

Brammer, A (2010) *Social Work Law* (3rd edition). Harlow: Pearson Education Ltd.

Brasse, G (2004) Conciliation is working. *Family Law,* 34: 722–5.

Brayne, H and Carr, H (2010) *Law for Social Workers* (11th edition). Oxford: Oxford University Press.

British Agencies for Adoption and Fostering (1992) *Developing your Court Skills.* London: BAAF.

Broadbent, G and White, R (2003) Identifying underlying principles in social work law: a teaching and learning approach to the legal framework of decision-making. *Social Work Education,* 22(5): 445–59.

Broadhurst, K and Holt, K (2010) Partnership and the limites of procedure: prospects for relationships between parents and professionals under the new Pubic Law Outline. *Child and Family Social Work,* 15(1), 97–106.

Brophy, J (2006) *Research Review: Child Care Proceedings under the Children Act 1989.* London: Department of Constitutional Affairs Research Series 5/06.

Brophy, J, Jhutti-Johal, J and McDonald, E (2005) *Minority Ethnic Parents and their Solicitors and Child Protection Litigation.* London: Department of Constitutional Affairs Research Series 5/05.

Butler-Sloss, E (2002) Expert witnesses, courts and the law. *Journal of the Royal Society of Medicine*, 95: 431–34.

CAFCASS *Annual Report 2009/10.* London: CAFCASS.

CAFCASS (2007) *Reporting to Court.* London: CAFCASS.

Children's Workforce Department Council (2009) *NQSW Pilot programme guide for supervisors 2009/10.* London: CWDC.

Civil Justice Council (2005) *Protocol for the Instruction of Experts to give Evidence in Civil Claims.* London: The Civil Justice Council.

Cooper, P (2006) *Reporting to the Court under the Children Act* (2nd edition). London: The Stationery Office.

Cull, L-A and Roche, J (eds) (2001) *The Law and Social Work.* Basingstoke: Palgrave.

Currer, C (2007) *Loss and Social Work.* Exeter: Learning Matters.

Davis, L (2007) *See you in Court: a social worker's guide to presenting evidence in care proceedings.* London: Jessica Kingsley.

Department for Constitutional Affairs (2001) *Tribunals for Users – One System, One Service: report of the review on tribunals by Sir Andrew Leggatt.* London: The Stationery Office.

Department for Constitutional Affairs (2006) *Review of Child Care Proceedings System in England and Wales.* London: The Stationery Office.

Department for Education and Skills (2003) *Every Child Matters.* London: The Stationery Office.

Department for Education and Skills (2006) *Working Together to Safeguard Children.* London: The Stationery Office.

Department of Health (2000) *Learning the Lessons.* London: The Stationery Office.

Department of Health and Home Office (2003) *Every child matters.* London: The Stationery Office.

Department of Health and Home Office (2003) *The Victoria Climbié Inquiry: report of an inquiry by Lord Laming.* London: The Stationery Office.

Dickens, J (2004a) Teaching child care law: key principles, new priorities. *Social Work Education*, 23(2): 217–30.

Dickens, J (2004b) Risks and responsibilities – the role of the local authority lawyer in child care cases. *Child and Family Law Quarterly*, 16: 17.

Dickens, J (2005) The 'epitome of reason': the challenges for lawyers and social workers in care proceedings. *International Journal of Law, Policy and the Family*, 19: 73–101.

Dickens, J (2006) Care, control and change in child care proceedings: dilemmas for social workers, managers and lawyers. *Child and Family Social Work*, 11(1): 23–32.

Douglas, G, Murch, M, Miles, C and Scanlan, L (2006) *Research into the Operation of Rule 9.5 of the Family Proceedings Rules, 1991.* London: Department for Constitutional Affairs.

Dugmore, P and Pickford, J (2006) *Youth Justice and Social Work.* Exeter: Learning Matters.

Eccles, C and Erlen, N (2008) *Evidence Matters: Social Work Expertise in the Family Court: a handbook.* Totnes: Research in Practice.

Elkington, A, Holtam, J, Shield, G and Simmonds, T (2010) *Skills for Lawyers*. London: College of Law Publishing.

Ellison, L and Wheatcroft, J (2010) *Exploring the Influence of Courtroom Questioning and Pre-trial Preparation on Adult Witness Accuracy*. London: Arts and Humanities Research Council.

Freeman, P and Hunt, J (1998) *Parental Perspective on Care Proceedings*. London: The Stationery Office.

General Social Care Council (2002) *Code of Practice for Social Care Workers*. London: GSCC.

General Social Care Council (2005) *Specialist Standards and Requirements for Post-qualifying Social Work Education and Training: children and young people, their families and carers*. London: GSCC.

General Social Care Council (2008) *Raising Standards: social work conduct in England 2003/8*. London: GSCC.

HMICA (2008) *The family courts – the experience of court users*. London: Her Majesty's Inspectorate of Court Administration.

Hopkins, G (1998a) *Plain English for Social Services*. Lyme Regis: Russell House Publishing.

Hopkins, G (1998b) *The Write Stuff: a guide to effective writing in social care and related services*. Lyme Regis: Russell House Publishing.

Hunt, J (2010) *Parental perspectives on the family justice system in England and Wales: a review of research*. London: Family Justice Council.

Iwaniec, D, Donaldson, T and Allweis, M (2004) The plight of neglected children: social work and judicial decision-making and management of neglect cases. *Child and Family Law Quarterly*, 16(4): 423–36.

Jessiman, P, Keogh, P and Brophy, J (2009) *An Early Process Evaluation of the Public Law Outline in Family Courts*. London: Ministry of Justice Research Series 10/09.

Johns, R (2009) *Using the Law in Social Work* (4th edition). Exeter: Learning Matters.

Kemp, V, Pleasence, P and Balmer, N (2005) Incentivising disputes: the role of public funding in private law children cases. *Journal of Social Welfare and Family Law*, 27(2), 125–41.

Lamb, B (2010) *The Queen's English and How to Use it*. London: Michael O'Mara Books Ltd.

Larkin, E, McSherry, D and Iwaniec, D (2005) Room for improvement? Views of key professionals involved in care proceedings. *Child and Family Law Quarterly*, 17(2): 231–45.

Legal Services Board (2010) *The Future of the Legal Services Sector*. London: LSB

Lindley, B, Richards, M and Freeman, P (2001) Advice and advocacy for parents in child protection cases – what is happening in current practice. *Child and Family Law Quarterly*, 13: 167.

McBride, P (1998) *The Assertive Social Worker*. Aldershot: Arena.

McKeigue, B and Beckett, C (2004) Care proceedings under the 1989 Children Act: rhetoric and reality. *British Journal of Social Work*, 34 (6): 831–49.

Mantle, G (2001) *Helping Parents in Dispute: child-centred mediation at county court*. Aldershot: Ashgate.

Masson, J and Winn Oakley, M (1999) *Out of Hearing: representing children in care proceedings*. Chichester: Wiley.

Ministry of Justice (2007) *National Standards for the Management of Offenders*. London: The Stationery Office.

Ministry of Justice (2010a) *A Study of the Impact of Changes to Court Rules Governing Media Attendance in Family Proceedings.* London: The Stationery Office.

Ministry of Justice (2010b) *Public Law Proceedings Guide to Case Management.* London: The Stationery Office.

Ministry of Justice and Department for Children, Schools and Families (2009) *Preparing for Care and Supervision Proceedings.* London: The Stationery Office.

Munby, J (2004) Making sure the child is heard. *Family Law,* 34: 427–35.

Munro, E (1996) Avoidable and unavoidable mistakes in child protection work. *British Journal of Social Work* 26(6) pp793–808.

Munro, E (2008) *Effective Child Protection* (2nd edition). London: Sage.

NSPCC (2003) *The NSPCC Review of Legislation Relating to Children in Family Proceedings.* London: NSPCC.

Ofsted (2010a) *Annual Report 2009/10.* London: The Stationery Office.

Ofsted (2010b) *Children on family justice: a report of children's views for the Family Justice Review Panel by the Children's Rights Director for England.* London: The Stationery Office.

O'Rourke, E (2002) *For the Record.* Lyme Regis: Russell House Publishing.

O'Rourke, E and Grant, H (2005) *It's all in the Record.* Lyme Regis: Russell House Publishing.

O'Rourke, L (2010) *Recording in Social Work: not just an administrative task.* Bristol: Policy Press.

Partington, M (2010) *Introduction to the English Legal System* (5th edition). Oxford: Oxford University Press.

Plotnikoff, J and Woolfson, R (2009) *Measuring up? Evaluating implementation of government commitments to young witnesses in criminal proceedings.* London: NSPCC.

Plucknett, T (1956) *A Concise History of the Common Law* (5th edition). London: Butterworth.

Pope, D and Hill, D (2007) *Mooting and Advocacy Skills.* London: Sweet and Maxwell.

Preston-Shoot, M (2000) Making connections in the curriculum: law and professional practice, in Pierce, R and Weinstein, J (eds) *Innovative Education and Training for Care Professionals: a providers' guide.* London: Jessica Kingsley.

Preston-Shoot, M, Roberts, G and Vernon, S (2001) Values in social work law: strained relations or sustaining relationships? *Journal of Social Welfare and Family Law,* 23(1): 1–22.

Prison Reform Trust (2010) *Punishing Disadvantage, a Profile of Children in Custody.* London: PRT.

Pritchard, J with Leslie, S (2010) *Recording Skills in Safeguarding Adults: best practice and evidential requirements.* London: Jessica Kingsley.

Quality Assurance Agency for Higher Education (2000) *Social Policy and Administration and Social Work Subject Benchmark Statements.* London: QAA.

Schofield, G (2004) The voice of the child in public law proceedings: a development model. In Thorpe, M and Cadbury, J (eds) *Hearing the Children.* Bristol: Jordan Publishing Ltd.

Schön, D (1983) *The Reflective Practitioner.* New York: Basic Books.

Shaw, I, Bell, M, Sinclair, I, Sloper, P, Mitchell, W, Dyson, P, Clayden, J and Rafferty, J (2009) An exemplary scheme? An evaluation of the integrated children's system. *British Journal of Social Work,* 39(4): 613–26.

Slapper, G (2011) *How the law works: a friendly guide.* (2nd edition). London: Routledge.

Smart, C, May, V, Wade, A and Furniss, C with Sharma, K and Stretitz, J (2005) *Residence and Contact Disputes in Court.* London: The Stationery Office.

Smeeton, J and Boxall, K (2010) *Birth parents' perceptions of professional practice in childcare and adoption Proceedings.* CAFCASS Research Conference paper. www.cafcass.org.uk.

Smith, C (1997) Mutual respect or mutual distrust: social workers and the courts in child care decisions. *Liverpool Law Review,* 19(2): 159–79.

Social Care Institute for Excellence (2005) *Teaching, Learning and Assessment of Law in Social Work Education.* Bristol: Policy Press.

Social Work Inspection Agency (2010a) *Chronologies: a practice guide.* Scotland: SWIA.

Social Work Inspection Agency (2010b) *On the Record – Getting it Right: effective management of social work recording.* Scotland: SWIA.

Solicitors' Regulation Authority (2007) *Solicitors' Code of Conduct.* London: SRA.

Solicitors' Regulation Authority (2009) *Consumer Research Study, 2008.* London: SRA.

Solicitors' Regulation Authority (2010) *Solicitors' Disciplinary Tribunal Annual Report 2009/10.* London: SRA.

Stanley, L (2004) Children's guardians and the local authority: managing disagreement. *Family Court Journal,* 2(2).

Thompson, N (ed) (2002) *Loss and Grief.* Basingstoke: Palgrave.

Timmis, G (2003) Lawyers' perspectives of public law cases. *Family Law:* 33, 174–80.

Tisdall, E, Bray, R, Marshall, K and Cleland, A (2004) Children's participation in family law proceedings: a step too far or a step too small? *Journal of Social Welfare and Family Law,* 26 (1): 17–33.

Wall, N (1997) Judicial attitudes to expert evidence in children's cases. *Archives of Disease in Childhood,* 76(7): 485–7.

Walsh, E (1998) *Working in the Family Justice System – a Guide for Professionals.* Bristol: Jordan Publishing.

Westcott, H (2006) Child witness testimony: what do we know and where are we going? *Child and Family Law Quarterly,* 18(2): 175–90.

Williams, B (1999) *Working with Victims of Crime.* London: Jessica Kingsley.

Williams, J (2008) *Child Law for Social Work.* London: Sage Publications.

Youth Justice Board (2009) *Making it Count in Court* (2nd edition). London: YJB and Her Majesty's Courts Service.

Youth Justice Board (2010) *National Standards for Youth Justice Services.* London: YJB.

Index